THE SPIRIT
OF THE
CHINESE
REVOLUTION

THE SPIRIT
OF THE
CHINESE
REVOLUTION

Lowell Institute Lectures, 1930
by
ARTHUR N. HOLCOMBE
Professor of Government, Harvard University

HYPERION PRESS, INC.
WESTPORT, CONNECTICUT

Library of Congress Cataloging in Publication Data

Holcombe, Arthur Norman, 1884–
    The spirit of the Chinese revolution.

    Reprint of the ed. published by Knopf, New York,
issued as the 1930 Lowell Institute lectures.
        1.   China--Politics and government--1912-1949.
    2. China--Biography.   I. Title.   II. Series:
Lowell Institute lectures, 1930.
    DS774.H6 1973   320.9'51'04   73-876
    ISBN 0-88355-070-9

Published in 1930 by Alfred A. Knopf, Inc., New York.
Copyright 1930 by Alfred A. Knopf, Inc.

First Hyperion reprint edition 1973

Library of Congress Catalogue Number 73-876

ISBN 0-88355-070-9

Printed in the United States of America

PREFACE

These lectures on the spirit of the Chinese Revolution were delivered early in 1930 at Boston under the auspices of the Lowell Institute. They are the product of an effort to interpret for a wider audience the results of investigations in the Far East for the Bureau of International Research of Harvard University and Radcliffe College, published by the Harvard University Press under the title, "The Chinese Revolution." Revolutionary China is a country which has proved a grave-yard for the reputations of political diagnosticians, and their fate should be a sufficient warning for those who would again venture to tell what is the matter with China, to say nothing of undertaking the more hazardous role of prophecy. But the importance of the question Whither China? to the rest of the world will continue to be pleaded in extenuation of the errors of those who strive for a better understanding of the Far East by the West.

A. N. HOLCOMBE

CONTENTS

THE SPIRIT
OF THE
CHINESE
REVOLUTION

I

SUN YAT-SEN AND THE SPIRIT
OF DEMOCRACY

WHEN Kipling wrote the familiar lines "For East is East and West is West, and never the twain shall meet," he was thinking of India rather than of China. He did not foresee the Chinese Revolution. Nor did he foresee the Russian Revolution and the Third International and the efforts of the Communists to make revolution a universal instead of a merely local or national phenomenon. The fact is that the East and West have met.

This fact is attested by a crowd of witnesses. It is enough to cite the Chinese revolutionary leaders whom I have listed for discussion in these lectures. Sun Yat-sen, the original leader of the Revolutionists, received his education in American and English schools and colleges. He married for his second wife a graduate of an American woman's college. He sent his son to the University of California. He stayed during his last illness in the hospital of the Peking Union Medical College founded by Mr. John D. Rockefeller, Jr., and his preliminary funeral was conducted in accordance with the rites of the Christian sect with which he had been affiliated. There was another funeral four years afterwards which was quite different, about which I shall have something more to say presently. Borodin, the most important leader of the Revolution in the stage which followed after the death of Sun Yat-sen, was born in Russia; but he grew up in America, gained his education in Chicago, learned his politics there, engaged in business there also for a time, and conducted his revolutionary operations in China in the English language. Feng Yu-hsiang is, or at any rate for many years was, an ardent Methodist. He chose for his wife a secretary of the Y.W.C.A. And if he is not now a Christian, he is still as strongly opposed to smoking, drinking, gambling and swearing as any ardent Methodist or member of the "Y." could desire. Chiang Kai-shek was not educated in America, nor has he, to my knowledge, ever professed Christianity, but his wife is a Christian and a graduate of Wellesley College. They were married by the head of the Chinese Y.M.C.A. and for a beverage he drinks unfermented grape juice. At least, that is what he drank when I lunched with him at his headquarters in Nanking, though there was wine for those who desired it. Both T. V. Soong and C. T. Wang are American college graduates. Wang studied at the University of Michigan and at Yale, graduating from the latter institution in 1910. He stood in the

highest rank of scholars, and in accordance with the
time-honored Yale custom, was entitled accordingly
to deliver a philosophical oration at Commence-
ment, a privilege which he, like most others who
have had the opportunity, considerately declined.
Soong studied at Vanderbilt University and at
Harvard, where he graduated in 1915, having
specialized in economics. I have looked up his record
at the college office, and while I will betray no academic secrets, I will say that his record affords no
comfort to those who pretend that high academic
rank bodes ill for future distinction. I lunched one
day in Mr. Soong's office at the Ministry of Finance
in Nanking, together with the other Harvard men
who held office in the Nationalist Government at
that time. All the principal bureau chiefs in the Ministry of Finance were Harvard graduates, and I
could not help but feel that the prestige of Harvard
was at stake in their conduct of the national finances. Besides Harvard and Yale, Columbia, Cor-
nell, Oberlin, and the University of California were
represented among the principal department heads
at Nanking at the time of my visit, while the subordinate offices were thronged with the graduates
of American colleges.

Further evidence that East and West have met
is afforded by the information concerning the education of the leading men in China. It is about sixty

years since Chinese young men first began going abroad for a modern education. It is estimated that by the beginning of the present century there were perhaps a hundred Chinese young men studying in Europe, twice as many in America, and three times as many in Japan. After the Japanese victory over Russia, which greatly enhanced the prestige of Japanese education in China, the number of Chinese studying there increased enormously. It is estimated that in 1910 there were 30,000 Chinese students in Japan, as compared with about 500 in America and 300 in Europe. The aggressively imperialistic policies, which Japan adopted at about that time, rendered her educational institutions less popular in China; but the comparative cheapness of living in Japan and the proximity of the country to the Chinese continues to bring to Japanese institutions large numbers of Chinese students. It is estimated that in 1927 there were 5,000 Chinese in Japanese schools and colleges, 2,000 in the United States, and 600 in Europe. One effect of all this foreign education is reflected in the pages of the Chinese *Who's Who*. Out of 750 leading men of China, whose biographies are contained in a recent issue of the Chinese *Who's Who*, 382, a fair majority of the whole number, were educated abroad; 196 received western educations in missionary colleges or other foreign institutions in

China, while only 172, less than ¼ of the total, had received the old Chinese classical education.

Perhaps the fact that East and West have met may be regarded as sufficiently established. I wish next to consider briefly the significance of that fact. Having quoted Kipling, the poet of Western imperialism, I will turn to Tagore, a poet of Eastern anti-imperialism. He may or may not be a better prophet than Kipling, but his words have a more modern ring when he cries, "the fact that the East and the West have met is the most important of all facts in the present age." From the Occidental point of view this may seem an excess of emphasis, but I have no doubt that it is a moderate statement from the Oriental viewpoint, and we must not forget that there are far more Orientals in the world than Occidentals. More significant to the Western mind is Tagore's further comment, "So long as it remains a mere fact, it will give rise to interminable conflicts. It is the mission of all men of faith to raise this fact into truth." That is the mystical Oriental way of saying that the meeting of East and West must lead to mutual understanding or it will lead to strife. To contribute to the growth of such understanding is the object of these lectures.

The Chinese Revolution is one of the most complex phenomena in history. It is no ordinary revolution. It is a whole set of revolutions going on at the same time. In the West we have experienced in modern times a number of political revolutions, beginning with the American and French and culminating for the moment in the Russian. The political revolution in China, from the overthrow of the Manchus down to the present, is not inferior in dramatic interest to any of these. In the West there has been also a revolution in industry, no less important than that in politics, which has extended over a period of between one and two centuries. In China a similar industrial revolution is taking place, and changes which have filled a century or more in the West are being compressed into the span of one or two generations. But it is not only in politics and industry that the old order is changing in China and giving way to a new. The ancient Chinese family system is also at long last on trial, and the prospect of a great social revolution must be added to the present reality of the political and industrial revolutions. The meeting of East and West has started revolutions likewise in art and letters and philosophy, and the venerable culture of the Far East is in the melting pot. Strictly speaking, one should not refer to the Chinese Revolution, but should say rather the revolutions. Only the plural number is adequate. But I cannot discuss all the aspects of revolution in China in these lectures. I shall devote

myself chiefly to one of them only, the revolutionary movement in the field of politics.

The factors which seem to me most important in
the present phase of the revolutionary process are
indicated in the subjects of the lectures. I have
linked each of these factors with an outstanding
personality in the revolutionary movement. I do
not mean by this personification of the revolutionary process to exaggerate the importance of men in
the course of events. These men are all striking per-
sonalities, but the forces with which they are associated are far stronger than any individual. The
strongest individuals have been borne along on a
tide, the strength of which they have had the merit
to perceive more clearly than others, without, however, being capable of altering the direction of its
flow. But the careers of these men furnish striking
illustrations of the nature of the revolutionary
process in contemporary China and facilitate an
understanding of events which at best are elusive
and obscure. And in the case of one of them, the
subject of the present lecture, we have a personality which has itself become a kind of political
entity. An appreciation of its significance is indispensable for any understanding of the further development of the revolution.

It has been said that the Chinese are of all peoples

the most rebellious and the least revolutionary. It is a significant paradox. Chinese history is full of uprisings and insurrections. The high stone walls, which surround or until lately did surround every Chinese city, as well as the lower walls of clay and mud, which surround the villages in many parts of the country, are mute reminders of the unbridled disorder and violence which appear to have been characteristic of the land (as of much of Western Europe also) until recent times. From time to time these rebellions brought about a change of dynasty, but, until the overthrow of the Manchus eighteen years ago, they always left the institutions of the country undisturbed. For more than two thousand years the political principles contained in the Chinese classics dominated the minds of thinking people, and the institutions in which those principles were embodied were accepted without question by the masses of the population. From time to time dynasties rose and fell, but the ancient political system always survived. In many respects the overthrow of the Manchus was merely a repetition of what had happened on previous occasions at the end of a dynasty. Ordinarily it would have been expected that, after a period of fighting and confusion, the strongest general would seize the supreme power and mount the Dragon Throne. The imperial crown would be awarded in accordance with the maxim,

To the victor belong the spoils. The revolution of 1911, however, was unlike all previous successful rebellions. Its leaders were determined that no one should mount the throne again. On the contrary, borrowing a phrase as well as an idea from the West, they announced that the sovereignty of the Manchus would be succeeded by that of the people themselves. For the first time in two thousand years the leading features of the Chinese state were to be changed. In place of what the West had generally regarded as a typical Oriental despotism, the Revolutionists proposed to establish a democratic republic.

According to the traditional Occidental view of Oriental despotism, nothing could be more alien to China than democracy. In fact however the government of the Celestial Empire was very different from that suggested by popular tradition in the West, and in certain respects the political traditions of China were favorable to democracy.

In the first place, under the time-honored system of local self-government in the cities and villages of the country, a large measure of power had always been reserved for the natural leaders of the people. In the villages, where most of the people lived, the aldermen and selectmen had the power in their own hands and managed local affairs in their own way. In the cities, the artisans and craftsmen were organized in their guilds, as formerly in the cities of

Western Europe, and the grandmasters of the various trades and the wardens of the different sections in which the trades were carried on exercised most of the functions of local government. The authority of the wardens and grandmasters, and of the selectmen and aldermen, depended in turn upon that of the heads of families, who, under the Chinese patriarchal system, were the ultimate depositories of power. It was a system of local self-government which made the empire a great aggregation of city and village republics, and these were as democratic in character as the family system would permit. The nature of the system is well expressed in an old Chinese folk-song, which sums up the state of mind, politically speaking, of these "farmers of forty centuries," as the bulk of the people of China have been rightly described. "When the sun rises, I toil; When the sun sets, I rest; I dig wells for water; I till the fields for food; What has the Emperor's power to do with me?"

A second factor, favorable to democracy under the old imperial system of government, was the method of recruiting the mandarins who actually administered the government of the empire. These officials were certainly undemocratic enough in their manner of discharging the duties of their offices. Affairs of state were not regarded as public affairs, but rather as private affairs of the emperor and of the administrative hierarchy composed of the mandarins. As long as the public received the services which they expected from the government, it did not concern itself with problems of imperial politics. Such matters were left entirely to the mandarins who were employed to attend to them. The public business was the private business, so to speak, of the mandarins. Their position was much like that of, say, stockbrokers in this country at the present time. As long as investors and speculators get satisfactory service at the customary rates, they do not care how the stock exchange manages the details of the business or whether stock brokers get rich out of the business. So it was with the mandarins in China during the old imperial régime. But, whereas a New York stock-broker gets his seat by purchase, the mandarin qualified for his position by competitive examination. The examinations were open to all on equal terms, and there was no village in China so humble but that a talented youth might hope by diligence and merit to secure a place in the government of the empire. Thus the masses of the population were as much interested in the maintenance of the system as the scholars themselves. Ambitious men, who failed to gain admittance to the official hierarchy, found it difficult to show that it was the system, and not themselves, that was at fault, and so one great cause of discontent and disorder in undemocratic countries was stopped at the source. The popular extraction of the mandarins was not only a source of strength to the imperial system, when it was in good working order, but also, because it prevented the growth of a privileged hereditary ruling class, a great bulwark of social democracy.

A third factor, making for a spirit of democracy in imperial China, was the character of the imperial office itself. The old Chinese empire is sometimes described as a paternalistic institution, but the relations between emperor and subject under the Confucian code were not at all like those between father and son. The patriarchal family was an absolute monarchy. The authority of the father over his children was not limited by any law other than that of nature itself. The Chinese classics furnish no sanction for violent resistance by a son to a father or for any form of filial disobedience. Rebellion, on the other hand, was the recognized right of oppressed subjects, if they did not obtain the good government which it was the duty of the emperor to secure for them. No emperor had any claim upon the loyalty of his subjects except that conferred by the mandate of Heaven, and what Heaven had bestowed it might withdraw at discretion. According to the classical political theory, Heaven would withdraw its mandate, if the emperor proved unworthy of his high office. Successful rebellion was accepted

as conclusive evidence that the Heavenly mandate
had been withdrawn. The Son of Heaven on the
Dragon Throne was no absolute monarch. He was
merely an hereditary chief magistrate, whose duties
were punctiliously prescribed by long-established
custom, whose powers were carefully defined by the
moral law. His business was not so much to enforce
his arbitrary will, but rather to set a conspicuous
public example of right conduct and obedience to
law. In the eyes of his people he was not merely the
mighty lord on the Dragon Throne, but also the
humble suppliant at the Altar of Heaven. Those
who know Chinese history may object that many
emperors were in fact unfit for the duties of their
high office and served their subjects badly. But this
does not destroy the democratic character of an
office, whose incumbent was popularly regarded as
the first servant of the empire with no better title
to his office than that conferred by good service
to his subjects.

The classical political philosophy of China, as
formulated by Confucius and his disciples two
thousand four hundred years ago, may be summed
up in a few simple propositions. The first is, that
the people should be governed by moral agency in
preference to physical force. The second, that the
service of the wisest and ablest men in the empire
is indispensable for its good government. The third,

that the people have a right to depose a sovereign who permits oppressive or tyrannical rule. The right of rebellion plays an important part in the practical operation of this system of politics. The refusal of the able and wise to serve the government was always accepted as a sign of weakness and a warning of imminent rebellion. Moreover, the inability of the government to protect the people against the consequences of unfavorable natural phenomena, or other circumstances apparently beyond their control, might be interpreted as a sign of neglect of duty by the sovereign and a justification for the exercise by the people of their right of rebellion. That the Chinese should be the most rebellious, though the least revolutionary, of peoples, is the logical result of such a system of politics.

Long before the overthrow of the Manchus it was evident that the Manchu dynasty had exhausted its Heavenly mandate. Their inability to protect the country against the invasions of the foreign Powers was in the eyes of the Chinese merely one of the signs of their unfitness to rule. The Manchus had manifestly degenerated during their long tenure of power. The mandarins also had become demoralized and the best and ablest scholars were increasingly reluctant to serve the dynasty. By all the accepted signs a successful rebellion was imminent. But thoughtful Chinese, influenced by the contact of East and West, were beginning to fear that no ordinary rebellion, resulting in a mere change of dynasty, would suffice. The establishment of a new dynasty by the time-honored methods, it seemed, would involve too much fighting and disorder. The traditional process for regenerating the empire at the end of an effete dynasty was too dangerous under the strenuous conditions of the modern world. Before the new dynasty could establish itself, there might be a partition of the country among the Powers. Moreover, thoughtful Chinese began to perceive that the old classical education was not equal to the task of restoring the morale of the mandarins. Knowledge of the new learning of the West would be necessary, if the mandarins were to be competent for their tasks under the new condition of affairs. Finally, it would be necessary to strengthen the foundations of the state, by giving the masses of the people a greater share of power, and thereby building up a greater sense of responsibility on their part for the proper conduct of public affairs. It would be necessary, in other words, not merely to change the personnel of the government, but to regenerate the state itself by refurnishing the minds of the people. They would have to learn to regard affairs of state, not as mere private business of the emperor and the mandarins, but as public business with which all good citizens should be concerned.

This, in brief, was the argument for a revolution, instead of a mere rebellion, to the end that a democratic republic, administered by men conversant with the new learning of the West, should take the place of the ancient scholastic empire.

Sun Yat-sen, the late leader of the Chinese Revolutionists, was not the originator of this argument for a revolution in Chinese politics instead of a rebellion of the time-honored kind. But he saw the necessity of a new political order more quickly and more clearly than most, and devoted himself to the cause of the Revolution with greater ardor and persistence. It was his passionate conviction of the necessity for a revolution in the system of education, the basis of the old political order, as well as in the form of government, and his invincible faith in the political capacity of the Chinese people, that inspired his life-long devotion to the cause. On this revolutionary platform he took his stand, and nothing could dislodge him. In his "Memoirs of a Chinese Revolutionary," written a few years before the close of his career, he said that neither the might of the Manchu dynasty nor all the misfortunes of his life were able to turn him aside from the course he had set himself. "I strove for what I aspired to," he wrote, "and the more failures I experienced, the more I yearned for the struggle." He reflected upon the success of the Revolutionists in overthrowing the Manchus

and upon their failure subsequently to establish a
sound republican government, and concluded that
the explanation was to be found, not in any political
incapacity of the Chinese people, as alleged by some
of the critics of the Revolution, nor in any indisposi-
tion on the part of the Chinese to enjoy the blessings
of good government, as alleged by others, but solely
in the great difficulty of knowing what the maintenance of a modern state required of them. "Understanding," he was fond of repeating, "is difficult;
action, easy." It was his invincible faith in the people of China, as well as his passionate devotion to the
revolutionary cause, that made Sun Yat-sen the
perfect hero which he has become in the minds of
Chinese Revolutionists.

The career of Sun Yat-sen can be rapidly sur-
veyed. He was born in the year 1866 in a small village not far from Macao in the section of China
which first came into contact with the West. A
number of his relatives had gone abroad in search of
fortune, like so many others in that section of the
country, and an uncle who had settled in the Hawai-
ian Islands had built up a prosperous business. Sun
Yat-sen, when old enough for a Western education,
was sent by his parents to visit this uncle, and spent
five years in Hawaii. These were impressionable
years, and the youth, coming under the influence of
English and American missionaries, gained a thor-

oughly Western point of view; so much so, indeed, that his uncle became alarmed, and at the age of eighteen Sun Yat-sen was sent back home, lest he lose entirely his respect for the ancient Chinese culture. But Sun Yat-sen could not be contented in his native village, and soon contrived to make his way to Hong Kong, where he entered the medical college. Here he spent several years absorbed in his medical and scientific studies. Upon obtaining his diploma, he settled down in Macao for the practice of his profession. He soon became convinced that under the then existing conditions there was little future for men with modern educations in China, and little prospect for better conditions until the Manchu domination should be brought to an end. Turning his attention, therefore, to politics, he plunged into the revolutionary career which was to occupy him for the rest of his life. In South China, where the people had never become wholly reconciled to the rule of the Manchus, whom the Chinese continued to regard as an alien race, Dr. Sun found many others of his own way of thinking among the members of the widespread revolutionary secret societies.

The defeat of the imperial armies in the war with Japan marked a turning point in the fortunes of Dr. Sun as well as in those of China. An unsuccessful attempt to overthrow the Manchu power in Canton

led to the death of many of his early comrades and
to his own flight from the country. For the next six-
teen years, from 1895 to 1911, he remained abroad,
sometimes nearby in Annam or Japan, at other times
in Europe or America. Throughout this period he
was the principal organizer of opposition to the rule
of the Manchus, and he built up a great following
among the Chinese bankers and wealthy merchants
and prosperous planters in Indo-China, in the Straits
and East Indies, and in America. Despite poverty
and regardless of constant bodily peril, he succeeded
in keeping alive an active revolutionary movement.
He was especially successful in firing the patriotism
of the students, who in growing numbers were re-
sorting to the universities of Japan and the West.
Endowed by nature with an eager and active mind,
he lived in a self-made world of ideas, which the
ardor of his enthusiasm transmuted in the imaginations of his followers into the land of their dreams.
From the unexpected success of the Chinese Revolutionists in October, 1911, until his death five years
ago, Dr. Sun struggled in vain to give substance to
these dreams. He died as he had lived, an agitator and
conspirator, a leader of revolt.

There has been much discussion of the real character of Dr. Sun. The truth is not easy to discover.
By the enemies of the Chinese Revolution he has
been described as a hopeless visionary, as a vain-

glorious trouble maker, and even as a mere disappointed office-seeker. In April, 1928, when the cause which Dr. Sun had led was on the eve of its greatest triumph, though its success was in many quarters still unexpected, I visited one of the leading statesmen of the first Chinese Republic, who had been Chief of the Executive Power at Peking when Dr. Sun went there on the mission which ended with his death. I asked him why Dr. Sun had come to Peking at that time and what he thought Dr. Sun had really wanted. His reply was short and explicit. Dr. Sun came, he said, to get a job. Weary of perennial agitation, as this unsympathetic statesman believed, and discouraged by continual failure, the unfortunate leader of the Revolutionists wanted, he declared, rest, with a position to which he could retire, if not with dignity, at least with the prospect of a competence for his old age. And so this crafty statesman planned to reward Dr. Sun with an innocuous sinecure, just as formerly Yuan Shih-kai, the first successor of the Manchus at the head of the government in Peking, had put him off with an empty title, as it seemed, in exchange for the presidency of the republic. But instead Dr. Sun found the peace which he desired in the grave. And now, as my informant saw it, more practical men than Dr. Sun had created a fictitious character for the late leader of the Revolution, in order to exploit his good name for their private ends.

I heard a different tale from those who had known him better. Old men who had been associated with him in his early poverty and obscurity, young men who had followed him through the vicissitudes of his later career, told of the fascination which he exercised over them. They observed his eagerness for knowledge, especially the new science of the West, his love of wisdom, not overlooking the old wisdom of the Far East, his faith in his countrymen, and his high hopes for China. What others called a stubborn and domineering disposition, they termed loyalty to his principles. Where others saw only foolish vanity, they perceived unselfish devotion to the public good. His last visit to Peking, which seemed to soldier-politicians of the old school a confession of defeat, demonstrated in their eyes his invincible faith in the power of reason and his antipathy to the needless effusion of blood.

Those who knew him best held the highest opinion of his worth. Dr. Cantlie, his teacher at the Hong Kong medical college, who subsequently saved Dr. Sun's life when he was kidnapped in London by agents of the Manchu government, was a life-long admirer of his pupil. He wrote the first biography of Dr. Sun in English shortly after the Rev-

olution of 1911. Since Dr. Cantlie regarded that
revolution as the successful issue of Dr. Sun's life
work, he is evidently disqualified as an authoritative
political observer; for, as is now clear, the Revolution of 1911 was scarcely more than the beginning
of Dr. Sun's life work, and the successful issue lies
still in the future. But all the evidence inspires confidence in Dr. Cantlie as a judge of human character. After Dr. Sun had graduated from the Hong
Kong medical college and settled at Macao for the
practice of his profession, Dr. Cantlie used to go
over there to help his former pupil in major surgical
operations, and he gives as his reason for such unusual service that "he loved and respected him." Dr.
Cantlie specifies Dr. Sun's strength of character,
earnestness of purpose, and modesty of mind as the
secret of his great power over his followers; and in
another place he speaks of "his sweetness of disposition, his courtesy, his consideration for others, his
interesting conversation, and his gracious demeanor." Judge Lineburger, the author of another
biography in English written after Dr. Sun's death,
was as well suited to judge of the character of the
man during the latter part of his career as was Dr.
Cantlie during the earlier period. Judge Lineburger
especially notes his silence when he had anything to
gain by listening, his eloquence, when speaking before crowds of his followers, and his charitableness.

He speaks of him as prodigally endowed with moral strength, and, like Dr. Cantlie, ascribes his great influence as much to the force of his character as to the cogency of his arguments and the power of his ideals.

I once visited the house in Shanghai which Dr. Sun's grateful admirers presented to him and, lingering for a while in his library, turned the pages of the books he had once owned and loved to read. He was a voracious reader, and it was his practice to carry a book with him wherever he went. He read even while he took his daily constitutional in the neighboring park. I examined the notations he had made on the margins of the pages in his copy of Justice Oliver Wendell Holmes's famous essay on the Common Law, and I observed that he had read with similar care much of Pollock and Maitland's History and other weighty volumes dear to the hearts of Western lawyers and students of the science of government. It was evident that there was solid substance in this man. There can be no doubt that, while the spirit of the Chinese Revolution lives, Dr. Sun will be known as his disciples have portrayed him.

Dr. Sun has become the personification of indestructible faith in the political capacity of the Chinese people. His last will and testament, signed in Peking shortly before his death, bequeathed this faith as his chief legacy to the people of China. For forty years he had devoted himself to the cause of the people's revolution, the will began by saying, "with but one end in view, the elevation of China to a position of freedom and equality among the nations." The end of the struggle was not then in sight, but the will gives no sign of any loss of faith. Dr. Sun's last thoughts were concerned only with the choice of means. "My experiences during these forty years," the will reads, "have firmly convinced me, that to attain this goal we must bring about a thorough awakening of our own people." Dr. Sun was also convinced that there should be an alliance with those other peoples of the world, who treated the Chinese on the basis of equality. His faith was not confined to his fellow countrymen. He believed that peoples everywhere, who believed in themselves, would also believe in China and join in a common struggle for the dignity of nations. This is the profession of faith which his followers have been taught to repeat at the opening of every public meeting in Nationalist China. It is recited by public officials at their weekly assemblies, by all politicians at their conferences and conventions, by school children at the opening session of the public schools each Monday morning, and by the people at large on all patriotic holidays. Dr. Sun's portrait hangs in the most conspicuous position in every public hall and meeting place in Nationalist China, where all who attend can look upon his face, while they repeat the words of his will and devote two or three minutes to silent meditation.

The new faith in the political capacity of the Chinese people has been provided, not only with a ritual, but also with suitable places for worship. Its temples are the monuments to the late revolutionary leader which mark the spread of the Revolution over the land. These monuments have taken characteristic forms. In many places new municipal parks and playgrounds attest the revolutionary spirit. In some places also museums and libraries have been established in his name, where collections of patriotic literature and art serve the double purpose of commemorating the founder of the faith and propagating his gospel. One of the most significant exhibitions of this propensity for combining the sentimental and the practical is the giving of his name to the state universities under the Revolutionists' control. Respect for learning and reverence for the dead reinforce one another, making this, in the eyes of patriotic Chinese, among the most appropriate memorials to their hero.

More satisfactory perhaps in Western eyes are the monuments especially designed for memorial purposes. The most impressive of these is the great mausoleum on the side of Purple Mountain, overlooking

Nanking. It was Dr. Sun's wish that his body be buried near the city which he hoped would be the future capital of the Chinese Republic. The knoll on the mountain which was selected for the site of the mausoleum offered a splendid opportunity for a monument in the grand manner prescribed by the traditions of the country. Patriotic Revolutionists, mindful of the monuments erected by grateful peoples to the great men of other countries, the Washington and Lincoln monuments in our own country, Westminster Abbey in London, the Pantheon and the Invalides at Paris, and the beautiful memorials to the Tokugawa Shoguns at Nikko in Japan, as well as the famous Ming and Manchu tombs in their own country, were determined to build a monument which would bear comparison with any of these. An ambitious plan was chosen by open competition. Within a few months after Dr. Sun's death, work was begun, and through all the turmoil and confusion of the following years, work was never abandoned, though several times hindered by fighting in the neighborhood. Hundreds of men were employed, and in the spring of 1929 the monument was completed. The memorial hall and tomb, which together form the main edifice of the monument, are visible from the plain miles away. The magnificent structure stands at the head of a great flight of stone stairs, leading up the mountain from the end of a broad memorial highway, which connects the tomb with the city of Nanking. The hall is a translation of the traditional Chinese memorial architecture into concrete, granite, and marble, and will shelter the heroic statue of Sun Yat-sen, seated like that of Lincoln in the memorial in Washington. The tomb, which the visitor enters from the hall, seems from the outside to be of the type that is customary in China, but within is so arranged that the sarcophagus can be viewed from above, like Grant's tomb in New York or Napoleon's in Paris. The mausoleum as a whole is a triumphant expression of the spirit of the new China. The revolutionary leaders intended to build a monument which could bear comparison with the finest products of patriotic sentiment in the countries of the West, and they accomplished their purpose. It takes its place as one of the grandest and most beautiful of its kind in the world. It is a monument not only to the faith of Dr. Sun in the people of China, but also to that of the Chinese people in themselves.

Here, on June 1st, 1929, the body of the father of the Chinese Revolution was laid in its last resting place in the presence of the leading members of the National Government at Nanking, together with the surviving relatives and old friends, and the members of the diplomatic corps and other representatives of the Powers. Outside the memorial hall a great throng had gathered. Promptly at noon there was a profound silence. Throughout the city of Nanking, throughout all China, throughout the whole world, wherever patriotic Chinese could gather together, there was a similar silence of reverent multitudes. During three minutes the silence continued. Then the solemn rites ended.

A writer in an American newspaper published in China well described the significance of the event. "These past four years," he wrote, "have seen Sun Yat-sen transformed from a starkly determined but fallible revolutionary leader into the all-wise founder and guiding spirit of the revolution before whom all should bow and to whom all should turn for guidance and inspiration. Other men, after their deaths, have been transformed in much the same way and have become symbols of unity and loyalty, around which political or social or religious movements have turned. No man has caught and held people's imaginations, however, who did not have within himself certain great qualities of moral courage and unselfish devotion to what he saw as the right. These qualities Sun Yat-sen had and it was his possession of them to a rare degree which made him the force he was while alive, and the greater force after he died. It is no small gain to China that it should have acquired such a symbol to which all eyes can turn as the transformed Sun Yat-sen has become.

Through the centuries the tangible and visible symbol of the imperial throne served as the focal point
for such sense of national unity as existed. With the
establishment of the republic this symbol disappeared and there was nothing to take its place. Affairs were in the hands of ordinary men, behind
whom stood no semi-mystic authority in whose
name they could speak. That lack of a unifying symbol was one of the serious handicaps of the efforts
to get the new régime going. In these four years
since he died, Dr. Sun has come in no small measure
to supply that lack. The governmental leaders can
and do speak and act under his ægis. They get from
that association an authority which otherwise would
not be theirs. Though some of them may misuse that
authority, the fact that the authority is there is no
small gain. These men, too, by using his name force
comparisons between themselves and him, comparisons which help to hold them up to higher standards
and which aid others to judge them and to what extent they fall short of the high standards they profess."

We are now in a position to see what Sun Yat-sen
did for China. In the first place, he provided his
countrymen with a new symbol of national unity.
It is now possible for a genuine spirit of patriotism
to develop in lieu of the old spirit of submission to
imperial authority—the indispensable foundation

for the regeneration of the state. In short, the spirit of Sun Yat-sen has taken the place of the emperor on the Dragon Throne. Secondly, he founded a political party, designed to serve as the instrument for the new national spirit. The National People's Party, or Kuomintang, as it is called by the Chinese, doubtless falls far short of being a perfect embodiment of the spirit of the Founder; but it is much the most effective political organization in China, and may prove to be endowed with sufficient vitality to guide the revolutionary movement along the path which Sun Yat-sen designed it to follow. Thirdly, he gave the revolutionary movement a program for the reconstruction of the state. It is by no means an irreproachable program, but it is systematic and remarkably comprehensive. It will bear comparison with that of any of the great revolutionary movements of modern times in any part of the world. These are great services to the Chinese Revolution.

I shall not have time in this book to discuss this revolutionary program as systematically or thoroughly as it deserves. I shall have to stick rather closely to its political features, though it contains much of interest to the economist, the psychologist, and the natural scientist and engineer, as well as to the student of politics. And on this occasion I can only call attention to the most important features of Dr. Sun's political philosophy, leaving their further discussion to another time. The most important features are three in number. First, a theory of revolution; secondly, a theory of education; and thirdly, a theory of government. Under each of these heads, Dr. Sun made contributions of universal interest to the philosophy of the modern state. When the Chinese Revolutionists recite the words of his will at their weekly memorial services throughout Nationalist China, they are not only cherishing the memory of their late leader. They are also keeping themselves ever mindful of the great legacy which he left them, the most valuable part of which was his teaching, that a people which had lost its faith in princes stood to gain something of far greater worth, a new faith in themselves.

II

BORODIN AND THE SPIRIT OF
BOLSHEVISM

IN my last chapter I tried to show that there was
a well-developed spirit of local self-government
in China under the old imperial régime, and that
there were democratic elements in the government
of the empire itself. But the attempt to transplant
the institutions of Western democracy after the
overthrow of the Manchus failed, and the leader of
the Revolution, Sun Yat-sen died, as he had lived,
an agitator and preacher of revolt. The parliamentary republic, which had been set up after the revolution of 1911, was a sham, as Dr. Sun himself was
one of the first to admit, and the actual government
of the country at the time of his death, in so far as
it can be said that the country had a government,
was a thinly disguised military dictatorship. Young
Chinese returned from their studies in the West, or
graduated from Western institutions in the Far
East, found little opportunity for careers, for which
they were trained, and had little ground for hope
that opportunity for such careers would arise under
the existing political conditions. It was evident

therefore that the revolutionary movement would go on, even though Sun Yat-sen was dead. Indeed, as the event proved, his death gave it a new impetus.

The failure of the parliamentary republic tended to impair the credit of Western democratic ideas among the Chinese Revolutionists, and to increase their interest in alternative schemes of government, especially the various schemes for the establishment of a dictatorship of some kind. The most obvious form of dictatorship was that resting on military power and, as a matter of fact, during most of the period following the overthrow of the Manchus, military dictatorship in some form had dominated the political scene. But the Chinese Revolutionists could not be satisfied with the naked rule of force. Two alternative forms of dictatorship were offered. The first was Dr. Sun's scheme for a dictatorship by the revolutionary party, the Kuomintang, which he advocated as a temporary arrangement, while the people of China were learning what would be required of them for the maintenance and operation of a modern democracy. The alternative form of dictatorship, in the eyes of the Revolutionists, was a dictatorship of the proletariat, such as had been established at Moscow following the Bolshevist Revolution. This form of dictatorship was persistently advocated by the new rulers of Russia for adoption in all parts of the world. The Russian Revolutionists, so long as they were bent on bringing about a world revolution, were bound to be interested in the propagation of their ideas in China, and the conditions which existed there after the death of Sun Yat-sen proved extraordinarily favorable to the spread of their ideas.

In the first place, the plans of the Communists were aided by the death of Dr. Sun. While he lived there was no one among the Chinese Revolutionists strong enough to challenge his leadership; and the program for the political reconstruction of China, which he had always advocated, supplied the platform on which Revolutionists generally took their stand. Unfortunately, the particular plan for the establishment of democracy in China, which he had formulated, had been rejected by his associates at the time of the Revolution of 1911, and throughout the rest of his life he tried in vain to bring about its adoption. His great personal prestige among the Revolutionists prevented them from giving serious consideration to alternative plans for dictatorship, while he lived, but after his death the advocates of other forms of dictatorship gained a better hearing. The Russian Communists were not slow to take advantage of this opportunity, and proceeded to emphasize the alleged superiority of a proletarian dictatorship over the kind advocated by Dr. Sun for the next stage of the Chinese Revolution.

The second circumstance, which proved favorable to Chinese Revolutionists in general and the Chinese Communists in particular, was the renewal of fighting among the militarists in the year 1925. Sun Yat-sen's death at Peking put an end to any immediate prospect for the unification of China by agreement and the various military leaders who were contending for supremacy turned to fighting on a greater scale than at any time since the beginning of the Revolution. In the Northeast Chang Tso-lin, the Manchurian dictator, in the Northwest Feng Yu-hsiang, the Christian general, in Central China Wu Pei-fu and Sun Chuan-fang, and in the South various revolutionary generals, entered the contest, and in every quarter the military elements dominated the political scene. The growing confusion and disorder discouraged those who hoped to complete the Revolution by moderate measures and caused patriotic Chinese to turn more hopefully to the advocates of extreme measures. This provided a better opportunity than ever before for Dr. Sun's radical followers, who had seized power at Canton and sought to make that city the headquarters for the regeneration of China, and also for the Chinese Communists who, like their associates in all parts of the world, looked forward hopefully to good fishing in troubled waters.

The third circumstance, favorable to the spread

of Bolshevism as well as other radical revolutionary ideas, was the failure of China to derive greater benefits from the Washington Conference. The International Conference, which had been held at Washington in the winter of 1921–22, was planned partly to provide for the settlement of Far Eastern problems, but as late as 1925 there had been little improvement in the situation in China in consequence of its deliberations. The Nine-Power Pacific Treaty, adopted at Washington under the leadership of the American Government, from which so much had been hoped for by patriotic Chinese, had not been ratified three years later, and had no other effect in China than to produce a feeling of disappointment, and a growing suspicion on the part of the Chinese Revolutionists that the Powers did not mean to make greater concessions to China than might be forced from them by a strong and aggressive Chinese Government. Chinese of this way of feeling became increasingly discontented with the weakness of the Peking Government and with the contentiousness of the military dictators. The Four Power Treaty seemed to mean a combination by the principal imperialistic Powers against China and Russia. Meanwhile imperialistic writers began to discuss the partition of China among the Powers or military intervention in some form more openly than for a quarter of a century. Patriotic Chinese began to fear that the long deferred partition of China might come to pass; or that the unification of China under a military dictatorship could be brought about only under circumstances involving a virtual protectorate by one or more of the foreign Powers. These fears further strengthened the tendency to turn from moderate to more radical measures. This also favored the schemes of the Communists as well as those of Dr. Sun's followers.

A final circumstance, which marked the definite turning point from moderate to radical revolution, was the Shanghai massacre. This unfortunate incident took place on May 30, 1925, less than three months after the death of Dr. Sun. It grew out of a strike by Chinese workers in the Japanese cotton mills. A great street demonstration was organized. Communist agents apparently took part in arranging this demonstration and certainly were active in exploiting its consequences. The police authorities handled it unwisely. Shots were fired by the police into the ranks of the demonstrators. Twelve were killed on the spot and a larger number wounded. This slaughter was the proverbial last straw, which made the burden imposed upon the Chinese by the alleged aggressive policies of the foreign Powers seem intolerable. A wave of hot resentment swept over all China. Feeling ran especially high against the British. The government of the international settlement in Shanghai, where the shooting took place, was dominated by the British and the police officer who gave the order to fire was an Englishman. In many parts of the country demonstrations were organized to protest against the shooting. Less than a month later a procession of students and workmen was making a demonstration before the foreign settlement in Canton. Again there was shooting, and forty-four of the demonstrators fell dead or died later of their wounds. The resentment of the Chinese grew exceedingly bitter. In Hong Kong their trade unions called a general strike against British trade, which lasted for more than a year. The injury to British interests was very great. In vain the British pleaded self-defense in justification of the shooting. The facts were difficult to ascertain, and each side believed what it wished to believe. At last the Revolutionists had gained the ear of the people of China, and they made the most of their opportunity. Both Chinese Nationalists and Communists denounced imperialistic aggressions with unprecedented vehemence. Their leaders discovered for the first time the tremendous possibilities of such propaganda, while the British perceived too late that violence, however justified, had become unprofitable.

It should not be surprising to an American audience that such apparently trivial incidents should

produce such grave consequences. We can appreciate their political importance, because of our knowledge of the importance of similar events in our own
history. It is only necessary to walk down State
Street in Boston to the corner of Exchange, and
there we will see embedded in the pavement a bronze
tablet marking the site of the Boston massacre of
1770. That was an incident costing fewer lives than
the Shanghai massacre of 1925 but after more than
one hundred and fifty years we still cherish its memory and point with solemn pride to the spot where
it occurred. So it will be with the Shanghai massacre
of 1925.

The interest of Russian Revolutionists in the Chinese revolution dated from the beginning of the
Russian Revolution. Committed to the theory that
the revolution in Russia was merely the beginning of
a world revolution, in which the workers of all
countries would unite, for the purpose of overthrowing established governments everywhere and
setting up a dictatorship of the proletariat without
regard to race, nationality, or religion, the Bolshevist leaders were bound to look upon the Far East
as an extraordinarily promising field for revolutionary operations. Lenin is reported to have said in
1919, "The Occidental Powers enrich themselves by
the exploitation of the weak countries in the Orient.
At the same time, however, they arm their Oriental

subjects and give them military training. The West is digging a grave in the East for its own burial." But at first the Communist leaders in Russia were preoccupied with the revolution in the West. The aggressive policy of the Soviet Government in the West was checked by the defeat of the Red army in Poland and by the collapse of urban industry at home. The Soviet leaders lost some of their early enthusiasm for the conquest of power by the workers of the world and gained a new solicitude for the conquest of bread by the workers of Russia. The destruction of the capitalist system by military operations on the Western front was perceived to be incompatible with the procurement of capital for the development of domestic industry. Militant Communism then gave way to the new economic policy. This did not mean the end of the effort to extend the dictatorship of the proletariat, but it did mean a search for new routes toward world revolution. It meant especially a quickened interest in the spread of Communist propaganda in the East, where the Western Powers were more exposed to attack and less capable of defending themselves. The new Oriental policy of the Soviet leaders was aimed particularly at Great Britain, which had greater interests in Asia than any other Power and which the Communist leaders thought could be more gravely injured than any of the others by operations in that quarter. They believed also that injury to Great Britain, the foremost capitalist state in the world, would do most harm to capitalism everywhere.

The development of the new Oriental policy was marked by a series of significant demonstrations. In September, 1920, a Congress of the Oriental Nations was held at Baku. In 1921 a soviet republic was established within the territorial limits of China by a successful revolution in Outer Mongolia, and the following year the first Congress of the Toilers of the Far East was held at Moscow, with representatives from all the Far Eastern countries. The new policy of pushing the Communist revolution in the Far East was pursued vigorously in the following years. The Communist University for the Toilers of the Orient was founded at Moscow, and a special university for Chinese Communists, known as the Sun Yat-sen University, was founded in 1925, following the death of Dr. Sun. When I visited this university three years later, though Communist influence in China had suffered an eclipse, there were still several hundred students in attendance, and the training of propagandists for the spreading of the Communist gospel in China was proceeding with energy and determination.

In the course of time, the progress of events in the Far East brought about strong differences of opinion among the Communist leaders at Moscow.

These differences of opinion ultimately exerted a profound influence upon the development of Soviet policy in Russia. On the one hand, Trotsky, and Zinoviev, who was then the head of the Third International, believed that the rapid organization of world revolution was necessary for the success of the Bolshevist system in Russia. They demanded therefore an aggressive policy in China, designed to convert the Chinese Revolution into a Communist revolution at the earliest possible moment. These radical Communist leaders were indisposed to temporize for long with the Chinese Nationalists, or to subordinate the special aims of Communists in the interest of a united front on the part of all Chinese Revolutionists against the Western Powers. Stalin, on the other hand, and Bukharin, preferred a more moderate policy in the Far East, believing that the Bolshevist system might be maintained in Russia, even though there should be no dictatorship of the proletariat immediately in other parts of the world. They were more disposed to coöperate with the Chinese Nationalists for the purpose of attacking the Western Powers in China. Even though the establishment of communism there might be postponed, they preferred to keep their ultimate aims in the background, until the Chinese Communists should have converted Dr. Sun's revolutionary followers to their own way of thinking. Eventually, these differ-

ences between the moderate and the radical factions among the Communist leaders at Moscow led
to an open rupture between Russia and China as
well as between the Soviet leaders in Moscow, but
this rupture did not occur until the spirit of Bolshevism had exerted an important influence upon
the Chinese Revolution.

Russian interest in the Chinese Revolution was re-
ciprocated by the Chinese Revolutionists, especially
by Dr. Sun. He had always hoped for foreign help
in carrying out his revolutionary program. He frequently expressed his desire for a new Lafayette
and was slow to give up the belief that the help he
desired would come from America or one of the
other more democratic Powers. But after the World
War the victorious Powers clung to their special
privileges in China, and showed little interest in Dr.
Sun's revolutionary movement. The Germans, however, were deprived of all their privileges after China
entered the World War, and the Russians volunta-
rily surrendered most of theirs after the Bolshevists
seized power at Moscow. In consequence, Dr. Sun
began to look more and more to Germany and Russia
for help. In 1923 he entered into an agreement with
an emissary from Moscow for coöperation between
Russian and Chinese Revolutionists. In the same
year his followers regained control of Canton. That
was the beginning of the *entente cordiale* between

Moscow and Canton, which for the next four years was the most important fact in Far Eastern history.

It may seem strange, in the light of later events, that Dr. Sun should have entered so readily into a compact with Soviet Russia. He was not a Communist and made no secret of his opposition to it. Both parties knew that their ultimate aims were irreconcilable and that their *entente cordiale* could not last very long. But both could also distinguish clearly between their ultimate aims and their more immediate objectives. And they believed that they might travel the same road in pursuit of these more immediate objectives, not only without conflict but also with much mutual benefit. The Chinese Revolutionists wanted help in the military stage of their revolution, and were willing to take the chance that Communist propaganda might eventually prove more seductive than their own among the people of China. The Russian Revolutionists wanted help in their Far Eastern campaign against the outposts of the capitalist system, and were willing to take the chance that the regenerated Chinese Republic might prove at last to be an enemy to their world revolution rather than a friend. Each party sought to gain at the outset by utilizing the aid of the other, and each might hope that in the end the cost of that aid would not be too high. Indeed each doubtless expected to convert the other to its own way of thinking. Neither was deceiving the other. Neither was intentionally deceiving itself. Both parties knew what they wanted. Both knew what they were likely to get, at least for a time. Both were willing to play with fire, since both expected to be warmed but not consumed by the conflagration.

The first fruit of this compact was the despatch to Nationalist China of a man who must be pronounced one of the most extraordinary of the agents whom Moscow has employed in its revolutionary activities, Michael Borodin. Borodin had borne the name of Grusenberg, when as a small boy he was brought from his native Russia to the United States. He had shortened his name to Berg, when as a young man he directed a business school in Chicago. He changed his name to Borodin, after the fashion of the Bolshevist leaders, when he abandoned teaching for revolutionary politics. He served for a time, it is said, as an agitator in Mexico, and eventually turned up in Turkey as the representative of the Third International in camp of Mustapha Kemal. In Chicago he seems to have become acquainted with the realities of American politics, as practiced among the immigrant masses of great cities. In Mexico and Turkey he acquired an intimate knowledge of the politics of revolution. Though the Turkish Revolution was not an unqualified success from the Bolshevist point of view, its leaders had understood how to establish their national independence, despite the hostility of the Powers, and to secure a position of equality among the nations. These were accomplishments the secret of which the Chinese Revolutionists wished to discover. Borodin was supposed to understand those secrets. He was also qualified by nature, as well as by experience, for the part which he was about to play as high political adviser to the Chinese Nationalists. At all stages of his career he had manifested extraordinary energy and intelligence. He was, in addition, a man of unusual personal charm, poise, and force of character. It seemed that Moscow could not have sent to Canton a man better equipped for obtaining the confidence of the Chinese Revolutionists.

Borodin arrived in Canton in the fall of 1923. In coöperation with Dr. Sun he immediately set about the development of the new political policy for the Chinese Revolution. There were five leading factors in this new policy.

The first was the maintenance of the *entente cordiale* between Russia and China. This was the easier, because of a certain parallelism between Dr. Sun's theory of revolution and that avowed by the Communists. Dr. Sun believed that the revolution should proceed in three successive stages. The first was the stage of military operations; the second, the stage of political tutelage; and the third, the stage of constitutional government. The primary objective in the first stage was the conquest of the power. That of the second, the training of the people in the performance of the duties of citizenship. And only after the completion of this period of training would the revolutionary leaders attempt to lead their followers into the promised land of constitutional self-government. Thus the second stage is, in theory, characterized by a dictatorship of the revolutionary party, and, while that dictatorship should last, there would be no question of democracy. In the Bolshevist scheme of revolution there is a corresponding first stage marked by the conquest of power. The second stage is that of the dictatorship of the proletariat, a form of dictatorship which is different in principle from that envisaged by the Chinese Revolutionists, but which has for its purpose the same general object—the training of the people for the performance of their duties and the exercise of their rights in the better state to come thereafter, the promise of which is held out as the justification of the revolution. The coöperative commonwealth, to which Communists look forward as the third and final stage in their revolution, would seem to be different in various important respects from the constitutional democratic republic, which Dr. Sun's followers are taught to regard as their political goal. But since the *entente* between Moscow and Canton was arranged primarily with a view to the requirements of the first stage in the revolutionary process, it was not difficult for Borodin to divert attention from the ultimately different goals to the common road, which in the immediate future Communists and Nationalists alike might be expected to follow.

I have a report of a speech which Borodin delivered before the students in the famous Whampoa Military Academy, which was founded at Canton in order to train new leaders after the Russian fashion for the Chinese revolutionary army. In this speech he argued that Soviet Russia's greatest contribution to the Chinese Revolution would be its revolutionary spirit. He denounced the aggressions of the foreign Powers upon Chinese sovereignty, the corruption of the politicians of the old school at Peking, and the tyranny of the militarists. He declared that the plight of China was worse than that of Russia had ever been, and that the hope of China lay in Dr. Sun's revolutionary followers. He warned his hearers against false friends, that is to say, Western imperialists, who would fight against the Revolution, he asserted, when they perceived its true aim; and he concluded with an appeal to the young students in the military training school for loyalty to the Revolution. There was nothing in his speech about a class war, or a dictatorship of the proletariat, or any of the other stage properties of Communist propaganda. It was a speech, such as any non-Communist among the Chinese Revolutionists could have made, and one well calculated to promote confidence in Russian friendship.

The second of the leading features of the new revolutionary policy was the admission of Communists into the Nationalist Party. To bring this about was one of the principal objects of Borodin's mission to Canton, and it is a tribute to his political sagacity that he was able to bring it about without delay. In January, 1924, the Kuomintang, as the Chinese Nationalist Party was called, held a first national convention at Canton, and formally approved the admission of Communists without requiring any renunciation of their Communist affiliations. It was enough that they should pledge their loyalty to the Chinese Revolution and their willingness to work for its immediate objectives in accordance with the program of Dr. Sun. At that time the Communist Party of China was very small, containing according to one account not over one thousand members, but under the patronage of the Chinese Revolutionists it grew rapidly and three years later, when, with the removal of the headquarters of the Chinese revolutionary government from Canton to Hankow, Communist influence in China reached its greatest height, the total membership had increased to about fifty thousand. The rapid growth of Communism under the patronage of the Nationalists eventually caused the Nationalist leaders to fear, that they would lose control of their own revolution; but at first the revolutionary leaders at Canton, for the most part, welcomed this accession of strength, and were fired with a new revolutionary enthusiasm by the infectious spirit of the Communists.

The third leading feature of the new revolutionary policy was the establishment of strict party discipline. Previously the Nationalist Party had been loosely organized, but Borodin and the other Communist advisers insisted upon a rigid system of party enrollment and strict adherence to discipline. They also helped to reorganize the Nationalist Party, giving it a form much like that of the Communist Party itself. Provision was made for holding party congresses every second year, and for electing a Central Executive Committee to direct party affairs during the intervals between sessions of the Congress, and to supervise the conduct of public affairs by the Government itself. This Central Executive Committee was designed to hold a place in the new revolutionary organization at Canton much like that of the Central Committee of the Communist Party in the scheme of government at Moscow; and the Standing Committee of this Central Executive Committee was the Chinese counterpart of the famous Political Bureau at the Bolshevist capital. Finally, Borodin and the other Russian advisers brought about a reorganization of the revolutionary government at Canton so as to facilitate the party dictatorship, which the circumstances called for, both according to the political philosophy of Sun Yat-sen and that of the Communists. The new form of government was in fact a soviet government, not distinguishable in appearance from the soviet governments established elsewhere under Communist influences. But it should be noted that the soviet system of government is not inseparable from Communism, and of Communism there could be no question in the mind of Dr. Sun or of his loyal followers. After his death they adopted the forms of a soviet republic, but they retained in principle the revolutionary program of their late leader.

Fourthly, Borodin and his associates insisted upon the creation of a partisan army, to take the place of the mercenary troops upon whom the Nationalists had previously relied, and who had proved more than once most untrustworthy. The nucleus of the new army was the body of cadets at the Whampoa Military Academy, trained under the direction of a young Chinese Revolutionist, Chiang Kai-shek. Borodin introduced also the Russian methods of maintaining civilian control over military operations. The political department of the army was created with its agents in every brigade, regiment and company, and commissioners at army headquarters, as in the management of the Red army by Moscow.

The fifth feature of the new revolutionary policy was the organization of the workmen and the peasants. Originally the Chinese Nationalist Party was largely in the hands of the intellectuals, scholars and students and members of the learned professions, in accordance with the time-honored Chinese practice which regarded politics as the business of scholars and looked to the scholar in politics chiefly for political leadership. Soldiers had been necessary also, but they occupied an inferior position in the estimation of the scholars and of the public as well. But Borodin and the Russians insisted on giving strength to the revolutionary movement by adding to the scholars and the soldiers the support of independent labor and peasant organizations, designed to throw their roots deep down among the broad masses of the people. There had been no independent labor movement in China until after the World War, and prior to the coming of the Russians it had not been an important element in the revolutionary movement. Peasant unions had not been thought of, until the coming of the Russians, but after Borodin's arrival in Canton the organization of labor and peasant unions proceeded rapidly, and soon the labor and peasant leaders were able to meet the Nationalist politicians on terms of equality, and to secure a position of corresponding importance in the revolutionary movement.

The new departure in the revolutionary movement was followed by an unparalleled development of power and prestige. Canton became the most talked-of place in China. The energetic and intelligent young men, who manned the Canton Government, gave a demonstration of progressiveness and efficiency such as modern China had never seen at Peking. They made their capital a model of civic enterprise and, thanks to the anti-British boycott, which forced trade from its accustomed channels, an unprecedented prosperity for the merchants of Canton helped to reconcile them to radical policies, which at first they had viewed with unconcealed alarm. The revolutionary leaders made the delightful discovery that nothing succeeds like success, and preparations went on apace to extend their sway over other parts of China. This is not the place for an account of the Northern Punitive Expedition, which set out from Canton in the summer of 1926 and within less than a year brought the greater part of China to at least nominal submission to the revolutionary government. At the end of 1926 the seat of the Chinese Soviet Republic was transferred from Canton to Hankow, and it seemed that nothing could stop the triumph of the Sino-Russian *entente*.

The first few months of the Soviet Republic at Hankow revealed a consciousness of power such as Chinese had not felt since the Sino-Japanese war finally exposed the rottenness of the Manchu empire. The British Government sent out a new minister to China at this time with instructions to visit Hankow before proceeding to Peking. At the same time the British Government published a memorandum to the Powers, interested in China, stating that in its opinion the time had come for them to show more sympathy with the Nationalist movement. It proposed to abandon the policy of foreign tutelage of China, as defined at the Washington Conference, and to pursue a constructive policy in harmony with the altered circumstances of the time. In evidence of its sincerity of purpose, an agreement was presently negotiated with the Nationalist Government for the formal rendition of the British concession at Hankow to the Chinese and for its government by a local council under the authority of the Soviet Republic. The signing of this agreement in February, 1927, was the greatest diplomatic victory yet won by the revolutionists.

It was the zenith of the Sino-Russian Alliance. Nothing perhaps better illustrated the consciousness of power at the new capital of the Chinese Soviet Republic than the activities of the Kuomintang's coöperating organization, the associations of workers and of peasants and the Communist Party. The all-China federation of labor established its headquarters at Hankow shortly after the Nationalist Government went there, and in the spring of 1927 felt strong enough to hold a Pan-Pacific labor conference, attended by representatives of all the Far Eastern revolutionary labor movements. A delegation representing the Communist International Federation of Labor also visited Hankow at this time. Portraits of Marx and Lenin began to appear alongside that of Dr. Sun at the party headquarters and popular meeting-places in Nationalist territory. The peasant unions grew even more rapidly than those of the workers. By the spring of 1927 one of the provincial federations of peasant unions in the area under Nationalist control claimed five million members, and the total membership of all the peasant unions was estimated at twelve million. The Communist Party of China also established its headquarters at Hankow, and in May, 1927, held its national convention there. The Communist leaders coöperated closely with the government of the Chinese Soviet Republic. Several of them held high offices in the Soviet Government, though only a minority of the leaders at Hankow ever professed to be Communists, and Borodin's influence seems always to have rested more upon confidence in the soundness of his judgment than in the number of votes which he directly controlled in the councils of the Party and of the Government.

At no time had the prospects for the success of the revolution seemed brighter than in the early spring of 1927. Six months later these bright prospects had utterly vanished.

Time is lacking to describe in detail the collapse of the Chinese Soviet Republic. The causes of its collapse may be briefly indicated. First among them must be placed the activities of the workers' unions. The union organizations had been conspicuously helpful in paving the way for the advance of the Nationalist armies, but they aroused extravagant hopes which the revolutionary government found it impossible to fulfill. The Communist agitators had distributed copies of the Soviet labor code wherever they went and created expectations of increases of wages and improvements in the conditions of employment, which were impossible to realize in a country as disorganized as China. In the urban centers industry was thrown into confusion by strikes and lockouts, and the politicians were unable to maintain order. The results were disastrous, especially in Hankow. A great increase in the cost of living was accompanied by a rapidly growing volume of unemployment. The economic disorder stopped the revenues of the Nationalist Government at their source and prevented the politicians from carrying out their promises to the people. At last even the radical politicians at Hankow perceived that the Nationalist Government and the labor movement could not survive together. They felt forced to jettison the workers' unions in order to salvage their own sinking craft.

Second among the causes of the collapse of the Soviet Republic were the activities of the peasant unions, which proved even more embarrassing in the rural districts than those of the workers' unions in the cities. The revolutionary propagandists had worked out a program for the redress of the peasants' grievances and for the amelioration of their conditions of life, but as the peasant movement developed, its leaders tended to get out of hand. They demanded not only the reduction of rents, but also the redistribution of land. They demanded not only the limitation of the authority of the landed gentry, but also all power for the peasant unions. Finally they demanded arms, in order that they might make good their claims to power. These demands meant the destruction of the old order in the country. They went far beyond the program of the Nationalists, and could not be granted without jeopardizing the progress of the revolution. The excesses into which the peasant unions fell brought their own cure. Under the Chinese patriarchal system it was impossible to redistribute the lands without offending large numbers of people, and when the peasant leaders began to demonstrate their authority by the execution of unpopular landlords, there was bound to be a reaction. Parts of Central China were plunged into indescribable confusion, and everywhere the miscarriage of the peasant movement impaired the prestige of the Nationalist Party.

Another important cause of the collapse of the Soviet Government at Hankow was the threat to Chinese society, caused by the Communist attack on the patriarchal system. That is a system of society which is utterly incompatible with Communist ideas of class war and proletarian dictatorship, and is not readily reconcilable even with the more moderate Nationalist policy of peasant and labor organization. Borodin, who was extraordinarily well informed concerning Chinese economic and social conditions, was of the opinion that there could be no genuine socialist revolution in China for many years, but not all the Communists in China shared Borodin's moderation. The more radical Communists, following the lead of Trotsky and Zinoviev, were convinced that a socialist revolution could be brought about in a comparatively short time, and that the sooner the Communists seized control of the Nationalist Government, the sooner they would get the kind of revolution they wanted. These dissensions among the Communists made the maintenance of the alliance between the Communists and the Nationalists increasingly difficult, and eventually brought about an open rupture. This was the final cause of the collapse of the Chinese Soviet Republic. After the Nationalist leaders at Hankow turned against the labor and peasant organizations, they lost the support of the Communists, and without this support they were unable to maintain their authority over the generals of their own armies. Thus a new militarism arose, and before its final collapse the Soviet Government at Hankow had turned into an ordinary military dictatorship.

The collapse of the Chinese Soviet Republic ended the Communist influence in the Chinese Revolution. Borodin was sent back to Russia. The most conspicuous of the radical leaders in the Nationalist party also fled the country and found refuge at Moscow. The retreat of Borodin gave a dramatic touch to the downfall of the Communists. Shaken in body by the fever which attested to his three years' sojourn in the Chinese tropics, broken in spirit by the failure of his carefully laid plans, he took a chilly leave of the disillusioned politicians at Hankow and set out on the long and painful road across the Mongolian desert to the bitter safety of the Soviet dominions. When I visited Moscow a year later, he was there unhonored and without employment, a virtual prisoner in the Soviet capital. Meanwhile, the Chinese Communists had played a desperate game. In December, 1927, they rose suddenly at Canton, seized the city, and for a day or two were masters of the original home of the Chinese Soviet Republic. Overpowered by the forces swiftly mustered against them, their reign was soon at an end. Members of the Russian consular staff were implicated in the uprising, one being killed in the street fighting, with arms in his hands. Thereupon the Russian consulates were closed throughout Nationalist China. The representatives of the Soviet Union were expelled from the country, and the alliance between the Communists and the Chinese Nationalists was shattered beyond repair.

Though the influence of the Communists was eliminated from the Chinese revolutionary movement in the course of the year 1927, the consequences of that influence were important and far reaching.

In the first place, the failure of the Communists in China exerted a profound effect on the policies of the Soviet Government in Russia. The radical revolutionary policies which Trotsky had sponsored at Moscow were discredited, and Trotsky himself lost his position in the Soviet Government and before the end of the year was expelled from the Communist Party. Zinoviev, the principal advocate of the policy of immediate world revolution, was also discredited, and removed from his office as head of the

Communist International. Stalin, and the other re-
maining leaders of the Soviet Union, concentrated
more and more upon the domestic policies of Russia, and the theory of world revolution fell into a
subordinate place in the Communist system of ideas.

Secondly, the rupture between Nationalist China
and Russia disrupted also the Chinese Nationalist
Party. Its Communist members for the most part
preferred to follow Russian rather than Chinese
leadership, while the more radical non-Communist
members, though they abandoned the alliance with
the Communists, continued to look upon Soviet
Russia as a helpful ally and possible source of aid in
the further stages of the Revolution. The more
moderate Nationalists, however, became convinced
that the Russians were more dangerous to China
than even the Western imperialists and, reversing
their policy, sought to establish more friendly relations with the Western Powers.

A third permanent achievement of the Revolutionists during the period of the Chinese Soviet Republic was the break-up of the united front of the
imperialistic Powers in China. At the Washington
Conference, the principal Powers who had been associated in the World War endeavored to continue
to act together in their dealings with China. The
policy of the Soviet Government at Canton, and
later at Hankow, in singling out the British, as the

principal obstacle to the success of the Chinese Revolution, had compelled the British Government to modify the policies, adopted by the Washington Conference Powers. It now was eager to protect its interests in the Far East in accordance with its own judgment. The Americans and Japanese, who are the principal other imperialistic Powers in the eyes of the Chinese Revolutionists, were left each to pursue its own policy, and the united front of the Powers in China was completely destroyed. From the Chinese standpoint this was a great victory for the diplomacy practiced at Canton and Hankow. It was not particularly a Communist achievement, but it is inevitable that it should be associated in the minds of the Chinese people with the period of Russian influence.

Fourthly, the new methods of propaganda introduced by Borodin and his Russian assistants had aroused the political consciousness of the workers and the peasants and enlisted for the first time the masses of the people in the revolutionary cause. This greatly broadened the basis of the Revolution, and, although the peasant and labor unions were broken up after the collapse of the Soviet Government at Hankow, the awakened political consciousness of the masses remained a permanent contribution to the development of the Chinese Revolution.

Fifthly, it was under the Soviet Government at

Canton and at Hankow that for the first time the young men of China, who had received modern educations, gained unquestioned recognition by the heads of the government and found the road to power wide open. This was one of the most significant of all the developments in the Chinese Revolution which took place at this time.

Finally, the spirit of Bolshevism in China contributed greatly to the emancipation of Chinese women. The Chinese Nationalists, in accordance with their Western ideas, had always favored improvement in the condition of women, but they had been slow to attack the time-honored family system, and as long as that system continued, radical improvement in the condition of women was impossible. The Communists challenged the authority of the patriarchs, and insisted upon the right of young women to choose their costumes and their occupations as well as their husbands. The revolt of the young women of China from their ancient bondage has already brought about a new birth of freedom for women in the larger cities, where the influence of the new ideas has extended most rapidly. It has caused much shaking of heads among old-fashioned Chinese; yet it remains one of the most far-reaching, perhaps, of all the permanent results of this phase of the Chinese Revolution.

III

FENG YU-HSIANG AND THE SPIRIT OF CHRISTIANITY

I HAVE now shown how the Russian Bolshevists tried to exploit the Chinese Revolution in the interests of their intended proletarian world revolution, and how the Chinese Revolutionists tried to utilize the Bolshevists for the purpose of their own national revolution, and how both failed. But these attempts, though failures, left their marks upon both Russia and China. Now I wish to turn to another set of influences upon the Chinese Revolution, growing out of the meeting between East and West. These influences are associated with Western efforts to convert the Chinese to Christianity.

Christian missionary activities have been going on in China for several centuries. The first Christian missionaries to carry the gospel to the Chinese were the Portuguese, who made their way into the country in the sixteenth century. These first missionaries were Jesuits, and they were followed by other Catholic orders. Gradually they acquired influence with the governing class, and during the seventeenth century some of them acquired important positions at the imperial court. A controversy between different groups of Catholic missionaries, concerning the compatibility of the Chinese system of ancestor worship with Christianity, discredited all Christian missionaries at the court, and put an end to their influence among the old governing class. For the last two hundred years the Catholic missionaries have directed their efforts primarily at the conversion of the plain people, and have not sought to influence the rulers of the country. The Protestant missionaries came into the country at the beginning of the nineteenth century. The imperial court continued inhospitable to Christian missionary enterprise, and neither Protestants nor Catholics made much headway, until after the country had been opened up by force of arms. The victories of the Powers in the so-called Opium Wars broke down official opposition to Christian missionaries, and thereafter their activities developed more rapidly. By the year 1926, when the Communist propaganda in China first began to compete seriously with the propaganda of the missionaries, there were about twelve thousand Christian missionaries in China. Of these two-thirds, or perhaps more, were Protestants, and one-third Catholics.

The methods pursued by the Protestant and Catholic missionaries are characteristically different. The Protestants broadcast their appeal to all classes of

Chinese, and engage in a good deal of public speaking before promiscuous audiences of Christians and non-Christians. The Catholics, on the other hand, engage in very little public speaking before non-Christian audiences, preferring in general to approach those whom they wish to convert through friends, who have already been won to the Christian faith. They direct their efforts towards the conversion of whole families or even whole villages at a time, while the Protestants deal, as a rule, with individuals, regardless of their family connections. The educational policy of the two divisions of the missionary body has also been different. The Catholic missionaries emphasize particularly religious education, especially the training of children and of priests. The Protestants give more attention to general education, especially higher education in secondary schools and colleges. They open their schools and colleges to non-Christian as well as to Christian students, and appear content that their students should complete their education without conversion. The Protestant missionary movement is also to a greater extent than the Catholic a lay movement, and its members reproduce in China, as far as possible, the mode of life to which they are accustomed at home. The Catholic priests, on the other hand, settle among the people, whom they wish to convert, and tend to live under much the same conditions as those of the

Chinese about them. The Protestant missionaries try to provide a model of a Western Christian home for the Chinese among whom they work, even though that means emphasizing the differences between life in the East and in the West, while the Catholics are disposed to minimize differences with the single exception of the difference of religion.

The results of the missionary activities of Protestants and Catholics doubtless do not measure accurately the relative values of their methods, but they are not without significance. In 1926 the total number of Christians in China was between two and a half and three millions. Of this number, roughly, four-fifths were Catholics and about one-fifth were Protestants. The total number of Catholics and Protestants together amounted to considerably less than 1 per cent of the total population. From a strictly religious point of view, the success of missionary activities may perhaps be measured by the number of converts. From this standpoint it must be admitted that missionary activities in China have been disappointing. There are ten times as many Mohammedan Chinese as Christian, and the increase in the number of Christian Chinese is painfully slow. The young educated Chinese are prone to adopt the positivist attitude, prescribed by the Confucian tradition, and fundamentalist Christianity seems to be making little progress among the educated classes.

From a political standpoint, which is the point of view I have chosen to take in these lectures, any attempt to measure the influence of missionary activities in China must also take into account the importance of the persons converted in the government of the country and the general effect of missionary activities upon the conduct of public affairs.

Many of the leaders of contemporary China are Christians and the proportion of Christians among the influential Chinese is certainly very much greater than among the population as a whole. The number of influential Christians who are Protestants is much greater than the number who are Catholics, as would be expected from the differences in the educational policies of Protestant and Catholic missionaries. A majority of the heads of departments in the Nationalist Government at Nanking are Protestants, and among the subordinate officials in the Nanking bureaucracy the proportion of persons trained in Protestant educational institutions appears to be even higher. Among the military leaders however the proportion of Christians is much lower, and the number of Christians among the leading generals is small. Among them, however, is one of the most remarkable figures of the Chinese Revolution. Marshal Feng, formerly known by foreigners in China as the Christian General, and in recent years more commonly referred to as the so-called Christian General, especially by those who have disliked him, has played such an important part in the military operations of recent years and also in revolutionary politics in general, and has been so deeply influenced in many ways by Christian ideas, that a brief survey of his career is not only of interest in itself, but also throws much light upon the course of the Revolution.

Marshal Feng was born in the northern part of Central China in 1880 and was brought up in humble circumstances. Beginning as an untutored coolie, he soon turned soldier, as many another peasant's son had done under similar circumstances, and sought a precarious livelihood among the mercenary troops of the Manchu empire. Gaining the confidence of his superiors, he received a military education in one of the new style training schools in the North, where he attracted attention by his prodigious energy and capacity for work. Gifted with extraordinary powers of organization, he rose rapidly in the armies of Yuan Shih-kai, and after the latter's death was recognized as one of the most efficient commanders among the Northern militarists. Picking his way among the morasses of army politics, he eventually became a principal contender for the mastery of North China. Driven from Peking by Chang Tso-lin, the Manchurian dictator, in the spring of

1926, he retired through Mongolia to Russia, whence, after a season in Moscow, he returned with fresh determination, and, rallying his scattered armies, forced his way down the valley of the Yellow River, as many a conqueror in Chinese history had done before him. A big, burly, boyish man of simple tastes and sound habits, he presented a striking contrast to the ordinary type of Chinese military adventurer, and inspired his followers with a matchless loyalty, that gave him a great advantage over his rivals in the struggle for power.

In fact, Marshal Feng was no ordinary militarist. Shortly after the overthrow of the Manchu empire he was converted to Christianity—it is said, by John R. Mott, who addressed huge crowds on a trip which he made to China at that time. Subsequently he strengthened himself in his new faith by marrying a secretary of the Peking Y.W.C.A. Like most converts, he was ardent in his devotion and eager that his soldiers should become good Methodists like himself. With a rifle in one hand and a hymn book in the other, they offered a contrast to the armies of the other generals no less striking than that between the generals themselves. The Protestant missionaries, proud of their brilliant convert, hailed him as another Cromwell, and his fame spread abroad. But, after his return from Moscow, he incorporated many Mohammedans into his army, and was compelled to alter his policy in the matter of religion. Perhaps, too, his new devotion to the gospel of Sun Yat-sen caused him to lose some of his former interest in the teachings of Christianity; but it is incorrect to charge him with an animosity against all religion, such as was preached by the Communists. It is unlikely that Marshal Feng ever became a Communist, though many foreigners have believed that he did. And while he has avoided in recent years public profession of his Christian faith, he has continued to give his confidence both to foreign and to Chinese Christians in whom he had learned to trust.

When I visited his headquarters in March, 1928, his soldiers still began the day with song. As in their general's most vigorous Christian days, the tune was still that to which Christians sing their doxology, but the words suggested the propaganda of the Kuomintang. The song was sung before the soldiers could break their fast, and the words may be translated as follows:—

> "This food is supplied by the people;
> We all should work for the people;
> Imperialism is the enemy of the nation;
> Serving the country and the people
> Is our sacred duty."

This patriotic song was sung before all meals in lieu of saying grace, a custom once practiced in the

Marshal's army but now abandoned. Yet Marshal Feng adhered to the strict regimen which he had learned with his Methodism. His men might neither smoke, drink or gamble, and if his army was in consequence an uncommonly sober one, it was also uncommonly inexpensive to maintain. The Marshal set an example of the simple life, contenting himself with a single dish at his meals like his men, and while they strove to fit themselves for the duties of citizenship in a modern state by learning two Chinese characters before each meal, he sat up far into the night after his staff had retired, studying the books which he thought he ought to know to fit himself for leadership.

Physically, as he first loomed upon my sight in the doorway of the cottage which served as his quarters, clad in the simple uniform of the common soldier, quilted with cotton to resist the cold, he might easily have been mistaken for an American football captain dressed for play. Vigorous, alert, impulsive and companionable, the admiration of his followers needed no explanation. The only complaints I heard from those about him were that he would do too much of the work himself, not delegating enough of the details to others; that he would interfere in secondary matters, where subordinates should have been left to bear the responsibility alone; that he was too careful of his men, and sometimes missed opportunities, which less considerate leaders would have turned to account. But these faults, if faults they were, only increased the devotion of his followers. Their confidence in his leadership, their assurance of victory, were amazing in view of the dejection, not to say despondency, so much in evidence in other parts of China at that time.

For the lack of confidence, which existed in other parts of Nationalist China, Marshal Feng was himself an important cause. The devotion of his followers was matched by the distrust of his rivals. He was dominated by·selfish ambition, they said, and no man could rely upon his support without fear of betrayal. "We trust him," declared a member of another faction among the Nationalists, whom I met at that time, "only so far as it is to his interest to keep faith." Others confessed openly that they feared victory in the coming campaign against the North almost as much as defeat, since it would surely be followed, unless they misjudged their men, by a quarrel between Marshal Feng and the other leaders. Still others were known to be awaiting the day when the quarrel should break out, hoping to find better fishing in troubled waters. And there were some who professed satisfaction at the Marshal's dubious reputation. "China," they declared with invincible optimism, "needs a strong man, a dictator, and Feng is our strongest man. The sooner he whips his rivals the sooner we shall have peace." But when I talked with him at his quarters two years ago on the eve of the spring campaign, asking him what he intended to do, when the Northern Militarists should have been driven from China, he replied instantly and with every appearance of candor, "I will carry out the principles of the revolutionary party."

At the time of my visit, Marshal Feng's capital, the city of Kaifeng, one of the capitals of the Empire in the time of the Sung Dynasty, nearly a thousand years ago, was the most interesting city in China. I was especially interested in his political training institute, where he was training civil officers to carry on the administration of the provinces under his control, and in his village leaders' training institute, where he was training men to supervise the improvement of the life of the peasants in the villages. The former institute consisted of five divisions, one for the district magistrates actually in office, a second for police officers, a third for candidates for appointment as district magistrates or police officers, a fourth for public health officers, and a fifth for municipal self-government leaders. The district magistrates and police officers were brought in from the administrative districts, of which there were more than a hundred in Honan province alone, in groups of a score or two at a time, so as not to derange the system of administration, and received a short intensive course of instruction in the duties of their office. Their teachers were young Chinese who had received a modern education either in the missionary colleges of China or in America. The other students were young Chinese who apparently would have made excellent officers for Marshal Feng's armies, and the fact that he should divert them from military to political training schools at such a time afforded striking evidence of his genuine interest in better government. The village leaders' training school contained over six hundred pupils, six being chosen by the district magistrate in each of the hundred odd administrative districts of the province. The weekly program in each school began with a Sun Yat-sen memorial service on Monday morning, at which there was the usual three minutes of silence, followed by the recital of the will and the shouting of revolutionary slogans. Then there were speeches by prominent provincial officers and members of the headquarters staff. The program of instruction was varied for the different sets of pupils, but in all cases there was systematic instruction in Dr. Sun's political philosophy, in the strategy and tactics of revolution, in the organization and procedure of the provincial and district governments, and in the general principles of Chinese law, with special emphasis on the new western codes. Marshal Feng was particularly interested in the practical applications of modern science, and laid great stress on instruction in road building, forestry, public sanitation, popular pedagogy and rural sociology.

In connection with the village leaders' training institute a village nearby was utilized as a kind of laboratory. It was named the Five-Power Village, in allusion to the type of constitution favored by Dr. Sun, and was designed to exhibit all the improvements in village life, which Marshal Feng wished his village leaders to introduce throughout the province. The village was surrounded by a high mud wall, like all villages in Central China, mute evidence of an age-long struggle against brigands and bandits. Over the main gate its name was painted in bold characters, bright blue on a white background, and on each side of the entrance were suitable exhortations, similarly inscribed. "Down with the bad old customs!" was painted on one side, and on the other, "Build up a fine new village!" More specific exhortations were displayed at other points of vantage. One vivid poster urged the people to "Plow land, weave cloth, and read books." Another read: "Cut off queues; unbind feet; stop smoking opium." A broad main street lead through the center of the village, a model of cleanliness and order. The village temple had been converted into a community hall and coöperative store, where modern household appliances were on view and arrangements could be made for procuring tools and farm equipment of the latest design. Not far away was a model schoolhouse, where two young men taught the older children, while two young women cared for the younger ones and for infants whose mothers were engaged in the fields outside the wall. Marshal Feng, though engrossed in preparations for the spring campaign, was greatly interested in the Five-Power Village, and determined that it should be in every way a model for the province. "Our people," he said, "are chiefly employed upon the land, and the success of the Revolution largely depends upon its services to those who dwell in the villages."

Marshal Feng did not believe in waiting for the end of the military stage of the revolution, to begin the demonstration of the benefits which the Revolutionists had promised to the Chinese people. Although his energies were devoted primarily to the training of his armies and other preparations for war, he insisted that the civil government in his provinces should bear witness to his purpose to improve the condition of the people. It was not easy to do. In some localities taxes had been collected from the peasants by the militarists, who preceded him in power, for twenty years in advance, and the plight of the peasantry was deplorable. But his provincial governments were composed of vigorous and intelligent men, who surrounded themselves with honest and public spirited assistants. They imparted to the administration of affairs a degree of enterprise and efficiency which could not be matched anywhere in China. Nowhere, at the time of my visit, was the spirit of public service as strongly manifested as in the region to which his influence extended.

It would be illogical, of course, to ascribe all the constructive features of Marshal Feng's program to the influence of Christianity, but the Protestant missionaries rightly pointed with pride to much that he had done as evidence of the constructive character of the religious spirit which they were trying to introduce into China. The Protestant missionaries were not so certain, at the time of my visit to China, whether they should point with equal pride to the man himself as a specimen of their work. British Protestant missionaries found it hard to forgive him for his desertion of General Wu Pei-fu, the military leader to whom British interests in the Far East had looked for a time as the coming strong man, who was to unify China by the sword and make conditions more favorable again for British trade. And even the American Protestants had begun to wonder whether he could be regarded, since his return from Russia, as a reliable exhibit of the converted Chinese militarist. Many believed that he had become a Communist and an enemy to Christianity, and those who disliked both revolutionary agitation and missionary activity, of whom there were many in China at the time of my visit, had begun to dub him derisively the so-called Christian general.

I can affirm, upon authority which I believe to be entirely adequate, though I am not free to reveal it, that Marshal Feng was not converted to Communism during his sojourn in Soviet Russia and had not become a Communist down to the time when Borodin was expelled from China. There is no reason for supposing that he would have become one since then. He was not even a Nationalist, until after his return from Moscow. Then he proclaimed his conversion to Nationalism and announced that he would do what he could to bring victory to the Nationalist cause. His part in the military operations of the last few years can be more conveniently described in my next lecture. It will suffice to observe at this point that his army bore the brunt of the fighting in the final campaign against the Northern Militarists, and that his behavior since the triumph of the Northern Punitive Expedition a year and a half ago has left the mystery of his purposes and character as obscure as ever.

In the spring of 1926, when Marshal Feng was driven from North China and set out on his trip to Moscow, the Communist attack upon religion in China had fairly begun. This attack was not directed exclusively against Christians. The Commun-

ists objected to every religion, which they branded
as superstition. Their propagandists were fond of
quoting Lenin's remark that religion is the opiate of
the people, and they attacked it in all its forms as
one of the obstacles to the propagation of their own
faith. The Chinese Nationalist leaders were not originally concerned with religious matters. The revolution which they had in mind was primarily political
and only incidentally, if at all, religious. Some of
them, indeed, as I have said, were active Christians,
and many of them acknowledged their indebtedness
to Christian schools and colleges in China or abroad
for their modern educations. At all stages of the Nationalist movement its leaders had received much en-
couragement and moral support from Christian
missionaries in China, and from their friends in the
countries from which they came. In some countries,
particularly in the United States, the sympathetic
attitude of the Christian missionaries had exerted
an important influence upon the policy of the government towards China. But not all missionaries
were equally sympathetic with the aspirations of the
Nationalists, and there was some impatience among
the latter when the missionary bodies, including even
the most sympathetic ones, hesitated to give formal
endorsement to the Nationalist cause and plunge ac-
tively into revolutionary politics. And so the Nationalists did not at first make much effort to oppose the

anti-religious tendencies of the Communist propaganda. The Communists, logically enough upon their own principles, attacked Buddhists and even Confucianists as well as Christians. Buddhist temples were frequently confiscated by the Nationalists, as their armies advanced, and occasionally a temple of Confucius was seized or even destroyed. But the Communists were especially hostile to Christianity on account of its connection with the imperialistic Powers. They stigmatized the missionaries as "hunting dogs" of the imperialists, and, though they were careful to distinguish between missionaries from countries whose governments recognized the equal position of China among the Powers, like Germany, and other missionaries, their propaganda proved very injurious to missionary activities of all kinds.

The anti-religious movement developed rapidly after the Nationalist army reached Hankow. By the late winter of 1926–27 Central China was growing hot for those missionaries who were most closely associated, in revolutionary eyes, with imperialistic Powers, and a few of them had been forced to evacuate their stations. The retirement of the missionaries was accelerated by the Nanking incident of March 24, 1927. Though only seven foreigners were actually killed in that unfortunate affair, among them were American, French and Italian missionaries, and the missionary properties in Nanking as well as those of imperialistic business men were thoroughly looted. A year later I could still see the abandoned houses of missionaries, from which every movable thing of value had been stripped, even to the window frames and floor boards.

There has been much controversy concerning the real responsibility for the Nanking incident. A wholly satisfactory explanation has not yet appeared. Those most in sympathy with the Nationalist leadership, as it then was, tended to belittle the incident as an accident, and those most opposed to it ascribed to the revolutionary leaders an intention to kill larger numbers of foreigners, at least of those connected with the imperialist Powers. It is now known that the actual order to loot the properties of the foreigners in Nanking came from the chief political agent of the Nationalist Party attached to the principal army which occupied the city. But there is still dispute as to the extent of his authority from the revolutionary government at Hankow. My own view is that the Communist political advisors of the Chinese Soviet Government desired to intimidate so-called imperialistic foreigners at Nanking, but did not intend that there should be actual loss of life. The reason they wished to intimidate foreigners was to accelerate the abandonment of imperialistic privileges generally, and particularly to facilitate the seizure of the international concession at Shanghai.

They had successfully overrun the British concessions at Hankow and Kiukiang, partly by means of intimidation, and they apparently overrated the possibilities of further conquests by that method. But the whole truth will probably never be known. Only Borodin himself knows the whole truth, and even if he should make a public confession, there would still be the question whether to believe him or not. Whatever may have been in the minds of the leaders of the Hankow Government, the loose discipline of the Nationalist armies made it easy for incidents to occur, which the leaders would not have deliberately ordered and probably did not even desire.

The killing of missionaries and other foreigners at Nanking brought about a general retirement of missionaries from most parts of Nationalist China. By midsummer of 1927 five thousand out of the eight thousand persons, who had been connected with the Protestant missions in China, had left the country. Of the rest, fifteen hundred had taken refuge in Shanghai, one thousand in other treaty ports, where they could be protected by foreign gun boats, and not more than five hundred remained at their posts. The missionary activities on the part of Protestants from the so-called imperialistic countries were brought almost completely to a halt, although the Protestant missionaries from Germany and other countries, which recognized China as an equal, were in many cases able to carry on their work. Three of the thirteen Protestant mission colleges, and fifty-five out of one hundred and seventy hospitals in thirteen provinces, were closed. The activities of the Catholic missionaries did not suffer as much as those of the Protestants, though in many places they, too, were forced to evacuate their posts. Among the Protestants, those who had been foremost in the show of sympathy with the revolution, particularly the Y.M.C.A., seemed to be the worst sufferers. The Y.M.C.A. buildings in several cities were occupied by the Nationalists, and its membership everywhere greatly declined. It was on the face of it a tremendous disaster for the Christian missionary movement in China.

After the collapse of the Soviet Government at Hankow and the suppression of the Communists, the missionaries gradually resumed their work, but it was impossible to carry it on precisely as before. In some localities the management of missionary enterprises had been taken over by Chinese, and everywhere the question arose whether the work of the foreign missions had been as effective as it should have been. The damage to the morale of the mission-ary movement threatened to be worse than the actual destruction of property. Above all, the efficacy of Communist propaganda, measured by its immediate effect on Chinese opinion and practice, had been a rude shock to the more complacent of the missionaries.

To the missionaries themselves the rapidity and extent of the Communist triumph was hard to explain. Certain of its causes, however, now seem fairly obvious. In the first place, the failure of the missionaries to treat the Chinese as equals was in marked contrast to the policy of the Communists, who treat all people everywhere as equals regardless of differences of race, color, and other conditions. With the rise of Nationalist sentiment in China, this difference between Communist propagandists and Christian missionaries worked very greatly to the disadvantage of the latter. It is true that in the eyes of the church there is no distinction between souls, but in the actual administration of missionary activities the principal places of authority and honor were generally reserved for the foreigners, and the power to direct Christian institutions of all kinds was in their hands. Moreover, as pointed out, less than one percent of the people of China were Christians, and the missionary's attitude towards the non-Christians could not but be influenced by their classification as pagan or heathen. In general, the Christian missionaries came in closer touch with the Chinese than any other class of foreigners. More intimate acquaintance with them made possible friendships with individuals, based on mutual respect and admiration,

and tended to promote similar respect and admiration for the race to which they belonged. But missionaries, along with their many excellent qualities,
are subject to the limitations set by their occupation. To go uninvited into a foreign country, in
order to bring light to the pagan race which they
find therein and to save the heathen, implies a state
of mind conscious of superiority. Even though the
missionaries may be entirely disinterested and have
no other object than to promote the welfare, as they
see it, of those whom they go to save, the resulting
relationship is one which cannot be as acceptable to
any proud people as one based upon complete equality.

A second factor in the disaster of 1927 was the
ignorance of China and of Chinese culture by many
missionaries. The training of missionaries in their
home countries lays little stress upon the study of
social, economic and cultural conditions in the lands
to which they may eventually go. Their chief interest is in changing the culture of the peoples whom
they wish to serve, and, logically enough, upon their
own principles, they are more concerned in giving
those whom they wish to convert the knowledge,
which they bring with them, than in acquiring from
their prospective converts a knowledge of the things
which they wish to change. But the Christian missionaries have not only a faith to offer, but also in-

stitutions to establish, and the establishment of institutions in a foreign country requires knowledge
of the soil in which they are to be planted, and of the
climate in which they are to grow. The Russian
Communists, on the other hand, had every reason
to learn all they could about the country in which
they were working, especially its economic and social conditions, believing as they did that the policies
which they should pursue must be adjusted to the
conditions which they would find. They make every
effort to understand these conditions. One often
hears it said in China that Borodin knew more about
social and economic conditions there than any of the
Chinese, and whether or not there be exaggeration
in this statement, I found it to be true that the Communist universities in Moscow possessed much more
systematic and comprehensive information concerning the conditions of the Chinese people than was
possessed by any of the universities in China. This
superior knowledge of the condition of the country
and of the real state of mind of the people gave them
a great advantage over the missionaries, at least in
the earlier stages of their propaganda before the consequences of their measures could be fully understood by the Chinese.

Thirdly, the Christian missionaries were quite
properly preoccupied with spiritual affairs, while the
Communists concentrated their attention upon

material affairs. In ordinary times, when people in general have little expectation of great alterations in their material condition of life, they may be expected to find satisfaction in spiritual interests, but in revolutionary times, when high hopes of rapid and extensive improvements in the conditions of life are aroused, preoccupation with spiritual interests put the missionaries at a disadvantage.

Fourthly, the lack of unity among Christian missionaries was in direct contrast to the original solidarity of the Communists and tended further to impair the influence of the former. Strictly speaking, missionaries do not go out to a foreign country in order to make Christians. They go in order to make Catholics, or Presbyterians, or Baptists, or Methodists. The Protestant missionaries in general show no special interest in Catholic Chinese, and Catholic missionaries scarcely recognize as Christian a Chinese who has been converted to Christianity by Protestants. These facts sorely puzzle the Chinese, and in the face of the difficulty of comprehending the sectarian differences among Christians and the impossibility of becoming more than one kind of Christian at a time, they naturally wonder if it is worth while becoming a Christian at all. The Communists, on the other hand, at any rate so long as they are struggling for power and are not under the necessity of finding means to perform their promises, were able to maintain an appearance of solidarity, which tended to inspire much greater confidence in them on the part of discontented Chinese.

Despite the apparent triumph of Communist propaganda over that of the Christian missionaries in the spring of 1927, the superiority of the Christian gospel over that of the Communists, in the eyes of the Chinese, was soon impressively demonstrated. I have already alluded to the wrath with which the Chinese finally turned upon the Communists and strove to destroy them. The causes of the greater stability of the Christian missionary movement, compared to that of the Communists, may well give comfort to believers in the superiority of the Christian gospel.

In the first place, the character of the missionaries in the end proved a great source of strength to their cause. The Communist agent, like the Christian missionary, thinks himself disinterested, but his preoccupation with material affairs gives his propaganda a materialistic character. If he is not actually working for himself, he does work for the benefit of a special class, to which he himself belongs and in whose fortunes he hopes to share. The Christian missionary, however, not only gives himself for a cause, asking nothing for himself except the satisfaction of seeing his cause prevail, but gives himself without any expectation of material advantage to the class to which he belongs.

Furthermore, in the eyes of thinking Chinese, the character of Christianity is much more attractive than that of militant Communism. The classical Confucian doctrine is a doctrine of pacifism. Its political ideal is an ideal of universal organization, in which all people shall have their place and live at peace with one another. To people with such doctrines and ideals the Communist doctrine of class war, with its fostering not only of hatred between different members of the same state but even of the same family, is thoroughly obnoxious. The Christian doctrine of peace and good will, on the other hand, is much more congenial to the traditional Chinese way of thinking, and in the long run, other things being equal, is bound to secure for those who profess it a much more cordial reception than can be expected by militant Communists.

In the long run too, the many useful services, which the missionaries have rendered in China, are bound to count in their favor. Whatever the Communists might have accomplished had their influence continued long enough, actually, during the period of their greatest activity in China, they were engaged in destroying rather than in building up;

but the Christian missionaries continued, as far as was practicable, to operate their educational and charitable institutions. The mission schools brought to the Chinese not only some knowledge of Christianity, as understood by some one of the Christian sects, but also a knowledge of the modern world. The Protestant institutions also gave a considerable knowledge of modern science, and all institutions gave a working knowledge of some foreign language, by means of which the student could pursue Western knowledge further. The improvement in the teaching of modern science in missionary institutions in China in recent years has been very remarkable. I visited most of the missionary colleges in China and found that they had been building modern laboratories and equipping them with the most modern apparatus for conducting experiments, and manning them with teachers well trained for the teaching of science. It would be invidious to mention particular instances, since all were planning to do what the institutions most richly endowed had already begun, but the practical teaching and research in applied science and especially in agriculture was very impressive and encouraging. The health activities of the missionary organizations were also object lessons to the Chinese, who, despite their traditional suspicion of Western medical science, are learning to value at their true worth the splendid hospitals and medical colleges, which have been established in the Far East.

The prospects for the spread of Christian influence in China since the disaster of 1927 seem to be brighter than ever, but the promise of the missionary movement will not be fulfilled without important changes in organization and methods of work. Since the Bolshevist invasion of China it is necessary for the missionary organizations to put more faith in Chinese leadership, and to make vigorous efforts to adapt institutionalized religion to the circumstances of the country. Some of the missionary bodies have already begun this, notably, the Roman Catholics and the groups under the supervision of the American Board of Commissioners for Foreign Missions. It may well be that the future historian of missionary activities in the Far East will date a new era in the religious development of China from the catastrophe of 1927.

If we can be content not to try to penetrate the veil which covers the future, we can discern a certain analogy between the present state of Christianity in China and that of its most conspicuous convert, Marshal Feng Yu-hsiang. Feng, through his army, has made a solid contribution toward the conquest of power by the Nationalists, but at the moment he does not share in the enjoyment of that power. Indirectly, through his demonstration of the value of intelligent training and discipline, he has done more than any other Nationalist leader to establish new standards of efficiency and public service in China. Feng is perhaps even more important as a setter of standards for the new Nationalism than as a leader of armies. But he has not yet found a definite place in the Nationalist régime, and his independence of action continues to be of such a character as to recall the cynical definition of an independent as a man who cannot be depended upon. He may yet prove to be New China's strongest man, and if he should, he will enliven the pages of history with a career which for picturesqueness and originality will bear comparison with the most romantic. So with Christianity itself. It has made solid contributions to the thought and action of modern China, indirectly even more than directly. But its present position as an institutionalized religion is uncertain and its future obscure. It may be that the revolutions, which are taking place in China, will not include a revolution in religion; and yet no history of the Chinese Revolution will be complete, which leaves out the influence of Christianity.

IV

CHIANG KAI-SHEK AND THE SPIRIT OF MILITARISM

THE first impression which most foreigners form of contemporary China is that of a country plunged into hopeless confusion and disorder by a crowd of rival militarists engaged in an interminable struggle for power. The stronger ones seem to be striving for territorial aggrandizement and riches, and the weaker for a bare existence. But everywhere, so it seems to the newcomer in China, the struggle continues without much regard for the welfare of the people and without much prospect of an early conclusion.

When I first reached China at the end of 1927 most of the foreign residents, whom I met in the treaty ports, agreed that the disorder and confusion would last a long time, unless something were done to put a stop to the fighting among the militarists. Some said it would last fifty years, some a hundred, some said forever, unless foreign intervention put it to an end. Under such circumstances there was among foreigners, especially those interested primarily in trade, a great longing for the emergence of some strong man, able to establish order. Some foreigners believed there was little prospect of the emergence of such a strong man, unless the foreign Powers should undertake to pick a likely winner and back him with their money, and perhaps also with their military strength. The "strong man," such people said, alone can cope with disorder and violence, keep insubordinate classes of society in their proper place, impart the necessary energy to the governmental machine for vigorous exploitation of natural resources, and assure that distribution of honors and profits which will be most conducive to enterprise and prosperity. The fame of Mussolini had reached the Far East and stimulated the desire for wilful leadership in Chinese affairs of state. The Primo de Riveras, the Pilsudskis, the Pangaloses, and the whole crew of European military dictators, fired the imaginations of Far Eastern business men, in whose eyes distance, perhaps, lent enchantment to the view of European militarism, and the yearning for the "strong man" became more intense.

The best that can be said in favor of military dictatorship as a form of government, and also the worst, was said long ago by the Englishman, Walter Bagehot, in his essay on the English Constitution. "By the Dictatorial or Revolutionary sort of government," he wrote, "I mean that very important sort in which the sovereign—the absolute sovereign

—is selected by revolution. In theory, one would have certainly hoped that by this time such crude elective machinery would have been reduced to a secondary part. But in fact . . ."—and Bagehot proceeded to relate some facts familiar enough to his readers of a half-century before the World War.

In view of the widespread revival of faith in military dictatorship in recent years, it is worth while pausing a moment to reflect on the wisdom of Bagehot. "The representative despot must be chosen by fighting," he observed, "as Napoleon I and Napoleon III were chosen. And such a government is likely, whatever be its other defects, to have a far better and abler administration than any other government. The head of the government must be a man of the most consummate ability. He cannot keep his place, he can hardly keep his life, unless he is. He is sure to be active, because he knows that his power, and perhaps his head, may be lost, if he be negligent. The whole frame of his State is strained to keep down revolution. The most difficult of all political problems is to be solved—the people are to be at once thoroughly restrained and thoroughly pleased. The executive must be like a steel shirt of the middle ages—extremely hard and extremely flexible. It must give way to attractive novelties which do not hurt; it must resist such as are dangerous; it must maintain old things which are good and fitting; it must alter such as cramp and give pain. The dictator dare not appoint a bad minister, if he would. I admit that such a despot is a better selector of administrators than a parliament; that he will know how to mix fresh minds and used minds better; that he is under a stronger motive to combine them well; that here is to be seen the best of all choosers with the keenest motives to choose. But I need not prove in England that the revolutionary selection of rulers obtains administrative efficiency at a price altogether transcending its value; that it shocks credit by its catastrophes; that for intervals it does not protect property or life; that it maintains an undergrowth of fear through all prosperity; that it may take years to find the true capable despot; that the interregna of the incapable are full of all evil; that the fit despot may die as soon as found; that the good administration and all else hang by the thread of his life."

China had not lacked experience with the "strong man" type. The first president of the republic at Peking, Yuan Shih-kai, had possessed most of its traditional attributes. He was free from the load of honorable but useless learning, which over-burdened the cultivated mandarins at the close of the empire and rendered them unfit for the management of a modern state. He was also energetic, shrewd, bold, and unscrupulous. He staked his fortunes on the success of the iron hand by superior efficiency in the manipulation of brutal force, in the organization of official violence. He hoped to master the country as similar men had done before him, and he found favor in the eyes of foreign business men. They pronounced his efforts good and backed him with their money. But Yuan Shih-kai failed, and came to a miserable end. After him came a long line of "strong men," each feebler than the last, each destined to a more ignoble end. With each failure of the policy of the iron hand, confidence, especially on the part of foreign business men, in the ability of the Chinese to govern themselves grew fainter, and paradoxically the yearning for a "strong man" grew more intense.

At the time of my arrival in the Far East two years ago the last hope of that influential element, whose favorite form of government is the military dictatorship, was the Peking dictator, Chang Tso-lin. Chang Tso-lin's government was a pure military dictatorship, unrestrained by such vestiges of republican institutions as he permitted to survive. The possession of Peking, however, gave him recognition as the actual, if not the legal, head of the Chinese Republic. His ministers were consulted by the representatives of the foreign Powers in residence at the northern capital; his envoys were received at Geneva and permitted to speak in the name of China at the Assembly and Council of the League of Nations; but while he himself dreamt of mounting the

Dragon Throne, the propaganda of the Revolutionists was dissolving the foundations of his power be-
neath his feet. Altogether deficient in the Western
arts of self-display, he followed faithfully the Oriental tradition which wraps up power in a shroud of
mystery and conceals the weaknesses it cannot or
will not overcome. Amidst a glut of wine and
women and a dearth of song, he exploited his power
for the gratification of his passions, assigning the
actual conduct of affairs to more intelligent or per-
chance to more brutal men operating in his name.

One of these was Chang Tsung-chang, the dictator of the great province of Shantung, and one of
the principal commanders of the Northern forces in
the spring campaign which was then about to open.
It happened that I had the opportunity to dine with
an official party at his headquarters on the eve of his
departure for the front. The great hall of his yamen
was thronged with officers, both military and civil,
who had been invited to the feast, and the long board
groaned under the burden of expensive dishes. The
champagne began to flow before the soup was
served, while bevies of singsong girls and geishas vied
with one another to entertain the guests. Amidst a
torrent of wine and an avalanche of feminine pul-
chritude, the genial host chased away his forebod-
ings, if he had any, of impending doom.

They were a merry crew, these survivors of the

line of "strong men," who held sway at Peking just prior to the capture of the city by the Nationalists in the summer of 1928. Chang Tso-lin, it is now clear, fell far short of the measure of the capable military dictator or "fit despot," as described by Bagehot, and he was not long in fulfilling Bagehot's prophecy concerning the fate of dictators who are incapable. Before I left China he had duly lost his head by one of the most artistic assassinations in modern history. Nevertheless, despite their disappointing experience with military dictators in China, the elements which favored that form of government were slow to give up faith in the policy of the iron hand.

It might be supposed that the failure of Yuan Shih-kai would have offered convincing evidence that no ordinary military dictator can solve the problem of China. Yuan Shih-kai had every advantage which any military dictator could expect to enjoy. He succeeded to the supreme power in a country not yet broken by rebellion and divided among warring generals. He could count upon the support of the old mandarins, and at the same time was in a position to utilize the services of the young men with Western educations. The foreign Powers had confidence in his ability, and the great five-power loan gave him abundant means to establish his authority. But he failed miserably. With the further passage of time and the greater insight into the causes of the disorder and confusion in China, the magnitude of the task which confronted Yuan Shih-kai becomes more clear. It is not possible to say that he could have succeeded, even if he had adopted the wisest measures for strengthening his authority; but the causes of his failure have become increasingly plain and, if understood by those who believe in military dictatorship for China, would suggest the unsuitability of that form of government for such a country. Yuan Shih-kai was urged by the wisest of his advisers to build up the new republic as much as possible upon the old imperial foundations, utilizing modern capitalist methods to increase the prosperity of the country and modern science to increase the efficiency of its ruling class. But he rejected their advice.

In the first place, Yuan Shih-kai never believed in the republican form of government. He did not believe that the people of China understood either the rights or the duties of citizenship in a democratic republic. He did not believe that they were capable of asserting such rights or of discharging such duties, even if they should understand them. He did not believe that they would wish to do so, if they could. He spoke of the returned students' political theories with derision, and branded their faith in the people as the credulity of gullible inexperience. He visualized the people in terms of peasants and workers,

merchants and scholars. He knew that the old scholars for the most part clung to the old learning, the
merchants to their trade, the workers to their jobs,
and the peasants to their land. They were not interested in partisan politics after the fashion of the west,
and would not follow partisan leaders into the laby-
rinth of representative government. They understood the time-honored rights of family patriarchs,
of village aldermen and selectmen, of the masters of
the guilds and the executives of the chambers of commerce in the towns and cities, of the district "father
and mother officials," but they had no knowledge of
the rights of man. Hence, for the returned students
trained in the political science of the West, Yuan
Shih-kai had no use. The only Western form of
training for public service in which he believed
was military training. He gave much thought to the
training of military leaders, and his military schools
turned out large numbers of Western-trained officers. With these militarists he built up his political
machine. It was a kind of spoils system, by which the
men, who seemed to him most likely to be the victors
in the use of the new weapons, filled the offices in the
new so-called republic. Thus, of all the Western institutions which Yuan Shih-kai might have adopted,
he chose that which is of the least value.

At the same time Yuan Shih-kai had lost faith in
the traditional institutions of the old empire. The

ancient system of competitive examination for the
selection of public officers was allowed to fall into
decay. Though urged by some at least of his advisers
to replace the discredited system of examinations,
based on the ancient classics, with a fresh system
based on the new learning of the West, he preferred
a free hand in the filling of the offices, and employed
the patronage to break down the opposition of the
genuine republicans and to reward the faithful or
the serviceable among his own followers. The returned students found themselves for the most part
disqualified for the official careers to which they had
looked forward. Some of them, to be sure, he utilized in the diplomatic service, where their knowledge of European languages and politics stood them
in good stead. But the road to power was open only
to men in whom he had confidence; above all, to
those who had been trained in his own military
schools. He built his political machine with men who
were strong in the new faith in organized force and
official violence, but weak in the old reverence for
the authority of reason. Mandarins with nothing
but the ancient classical training, like the returned
students, found themselves in disfavor. Thus he
alienated the affections of the old scholars without
securing those of the new. If Sun Yat-sen and the
other leaders of the Nationalist Party, the Kuomintang, were visionary revolutionists, Yuan Shih-kai

and his fellow militarists were no less visionary re-
actionaries. They looked back to the period more
than two thousand years ago, when the first great
emperor unified the country by the sword and,
brushing aside the scholars, sought to establish the
Chin dynasty on the basis of a military dictatorship.

The revival of such an ancient form of despotism,
though supported by the new military technique
acquired from the West, was fatal to the morale of
the government. It was not necessary for Yuan Shih-
kai to persecute the classical scholars, as the first
emperor had done. It was enough to ignore their
claims for governmental preferment. The best of the
old mandarins strove valiantly to replace the discredited classical system of education with one more
modern, which would be capable of producing a new
supply of statesmen; but the dictator's interest lay
in training military rather than civil officers.
Though some progress was made in the renovation of
Chinese education, it was not enough to rehabilitate
the mandarinate. Yuan Shih-kai filled the highest
offices in the provinces with the graduates of the
military schools, vigorous and forceful men doubtless, but in most cases from the old fashioned standpoint uncultivated and rude and incapable of per-
forming properly the duties of their rank. They
were mainly a greedy and contentious lot, too often
bent on getting rich as quickly as possible, and ready

to fight one another for power as soon as the heavy hand of their chief should be removed. In view of these conditions, it is not surprising that the government of China under Yuan Shih-kai rapidly became more corrupt and demoralized than under the last of the Manchus.

This disastrous military dictatorship did not even have the compensating value of assuring the independence and territorial integrity of the country. In 1915 the Japanese imposed their notorious twenty-one demands by the threat of war, and Yuan Shih-kai's weakness was exposed to the world. When the death of Yuan Shih-kai, a year later, was followed by the disintegration of his military-political machine, the stage was all set for the confusion and disorder, which rapidly brought the New China to the verge of complete ruin. The weaker "strong men," who battled for supremacy, abundantly demonstrated their incapacity to succeed, where Yuan Shih-kai had failed. Ten years after Yuan Shih-kai's death Chang Tso-lin, the craftiest of his disciples, was master of Peking and a part of Northern China, but without hope of subduing the rest of the country to his sway. It was evident that military dictators could not be expected to reconstruct China without more intelligent methods than those which had ruined the last of the Manchus as well as the more or less strong men who had succeeded them.

Into the political confusion and disorder, which followed the practical partition of the country among the militarists, came the Nationalist movement with a new faith in the people of China and a new technique for the reorganization of their institutions. But the new faith and the new technique could not dispense with organized armies and military leadership. As Napoleon once said, a revolution is an idea which has found bayonets, and the revolutionary movement, though dependent for its strength primarily on the propagation of the revolutionary idea, has in its turn also produced a new crop of militarists. Of these, the most important heretofore has been the present leader of the Nationalist Government at Nanking, sometimes called the president of the Chinese Republic, Chiang Kai-shek.

Chiang Kai-shek is one of the youngest of the outstanding military leaders. He is also the one most closely associated with the Nationalist movement. Born in Ningpo in 1887, he became a follower of Dr. Sun before the Revolution of 1911, and remained faithful to him throughout the succeeding years. Forced to flee from China after the failure of Dr. Sun's revolt against Yuan Shih-kai in 1913, he passed the next decade in obscurity. For a time he was employed in Shanghai, but he managed to pick up the elements of a military education in Japan, and, when in 1923 he returned to Canton with Dr. Sun, he was selected by the revolutionary leader to go to Moscow and study the art of war, as practiced by the Red army. Returning in the following year, he was put in charge of the new military academy at Whampoa, where officers were to be trained for the Chinese revolutionary army after the Russian fashion, and at last had the opportunity to show his true metal. He began turning out young officers well trained in military tactics, fired with a firm loyalty to the Nationalist movement, and greatly superior in morale to the officers on whom the Northern Militarists had to rely. At first Chiang Kai-shek was a favorite with Borodin and the Russian advisers. His power increased, and by the summer of 1926 he had become the most prominent figure at Canton. Though still in his thirties he received the command of the so-called Northern Punitive Expedition, the force organized to overthrow the dictatorship at Peking and unify the country under the Nationalist flag.

Chiang Kai-shek was well qualified to lead what seemed to most foreign observers an utterly forlorn hope. When I first met him at his quarters in Nanking a year and a half after the expedition had set out from Canton and while still apparently a long way from its goal, he was almost overwhelmed with preparations for the approaching spring campaign; but he talked as calmly and deliberately as if he were at a tea party. Youthful in appearance, modest and unassuming in demeanor, he betrayed no sign of the burden he had to carry; yet it was a matter of common knowledge that he was contending against the proverbial sea of troubles. Shortly afterwards I met him on a Sunday afternoon out for a stroll with his bride of a few months, the youngest of the charming Soong sisters and, like the rest of her family, a politician of no less skill than charm. They were coming down the mountain behind the old Ming tomb, where they had been visiting the Purple Cloud cave, and as they sauntered along together, gayly chatting, they might have been the most carefree young couple in the whole city of Nanking. Some distance behind were his military aids, clothed in proper uniform, but Chiang himself was attired in a natty outing suit, the last man in the party to be taken for the generalissimo of the Nationalist armies. In Canton, when I was there, Nationalist generals appeared in public only in powerful motor cars with three soldiers on each running board, pistols in hand, fingers on the triggers. In the Northern capitals the leading militarists at the time of my visit did not appear in public at all, unless the streets were first cleared. But Chiang Kai-shek at that time—subsequently conditions changed—could go on foot in his capital like any honest citizen.

Under this placid and serene exterior the Nationalist generalissimo concealed a stout heart and a strong will. With few words but firm purpose, he drove ahead at his objective, undismayed by the most formidable obstacles, the opposition of numerous and powerful enemies, the doubts and hesitations of timid friends. I met him for the last time at luncheon amidst a delegation of Chinese bankers from Shanghai, summoned to help finance the approaching campaign. It was a simple meal, served partly in the Chinese and partly in the Western style. Doubtless at the moment an appearance of economy was good policy, but simple as was the meal served to his guests, he contented himself with still more frugal fare; and while for the guests, a light wine was provided in addition to the inevitable tea, for himself there was unfermented grape juice of a well known American make. He appeared to be a quiet man of far from powerful, indeed almost frail, physique, and his friends often speculated as to how long his strength would hold out. It was a question as dubious in many minds as that other question concerning the loyalty of his greatest rival, Feng Yu-hsiang.

Time is lacking to describe the details of the now famous Northern Punitive Expedition. The first campaign began with the departure of the Expedition from Canton in July, 1926. The blue flag of the Nationalist Party with its big white sun in the middle and the red, white and blue flag of the Nationalist Government were solemnly handed over to the commander-in-chief at a great public meeting and Chiang Kai-shek made a well-advertised speech, declaring that the object of the expedition was to overthrow Wu Pei-fu and Chang Tso-lin and all other militarists and oppressors of the people, to unify China and secure for her an equal position among the nations of the world, and to establish governments in all the provinces upon the model of that at Canton. Covered by a cloud of revolutionary agitators and propagandists, who undermined the morale of the mercenary armies of the opposing militarists and sapped the strength of the counter-revolution, the Nationalist forces overran a great part of Central China before winter put a stop to the fighting. The revolutionary leaders transferred their seat of government from Canton to Hankow, while Wu Pei-fu was ruined and disappeared from the political scene. The unexpected success of the Nationalists was a great shock to the old militarists, and to their sympathizers among the foreigners in China. It foreboded ill to the old order in all its forms.

The second campaign of the Northern Punitive Expedition began auspiciously. When spring made the resumption of military operations possible, the Nationalist forces in Central China promptly finished the task of driving the Northern Militarists out of the territory still under their control south of the Yangtze river. March 24, 1927, they reached Nanking, which was hastily abandoned by the demoralized troops of Sun Chuan-fang. Meanwhile another Nationalist army had come up the coast from Canton and occupied Shanghai, which was also abandoned in haste by the demoralized troops of Chang Tsung-chang. One Nationalist army pursued the fleeing Northerners up the coast toward Shantung province, another advanced north from Hankow into Honan province. At this moment Feng Yu-hsiang, having returned from Moscow, and driven in the forces of the Northern Militarists from the northwest, hurled his army against their flank, and completed the conquest of Honan. In less than a year the Nationalists had overrun half the provinces of China and, including what they possessed at the outset, dominated the greater part of the country. These amazing successes were not won without hard fighting. The Nationalist officers trained at Whampoa showed themselves to be brave and efficient leaders, and the armies comprising the original Punitive Expedition never failed to give a good account of themselves in battle. But in the midst of the campaign of 1927 the dissensions between the Nationalists and the Communists came to a head, and the Nationalist forces were divided against themselves. During the second half of 1927 the Nationalists were hard pressed to hold what they had gained, and some of their gains were taken from them again by the Northerners. Chiang Kai-shek resigned his command and left the country, and the future of the Northern Punitive Expedition was full of doubt.

The final campaign, which opened in the spring of 1928, seemed to many observers little better than a forlorn hope. Chiang Kai-shek, having returned from exile, first reorganized the government at Nanking, then reorganized the forces in the field. Forming an alliance with Feng Yu-hsiang and Yen Hsi-shan in the Northwest, he sent his own army up the railroad which leads from Nanking to Tientsin, while Marshal Feng advanced up the Hankow-Peking railroad, and Governor Yen fell upon the flank of the Northern forces in Chihli province north of the Yellow river. The forces of Chang Tso-lin and Chang Tsung-chang met the attack on ground of their own choosing and for a time the fighting was sharp and the issue hotly contested. Then the Northern armies began to fall back and the retreat soon turned into a rout. The reoccupation of the Shantung railroad and of Tsinan, the capital of the province, by the Japanese, blocked the advance of Chiang Kai-shek and practically eliminated his army from the campaign, but could not save the Northern Militarists from ruin. Two months after the opening of the campaign the Northerners were thoroughly beaten and the Nationalists entered Peking.

Military observers were puzzled to account for the swiftness and decisiveness of the victory. Under ordinary circumstances it seemed that the Northerners should have won an easy triumph. But the circumstances were not ordinary. The propaganda of the Nationalists more than offset all their disadvantages of material and position. The Northern Militarists could not trust their soldiers. The soldiers had no confidence in their officers. The destruction of their morale was completed by the intervention of the Japanese. Thereafter no patriotic Chinese could give aid or comfort of any kind to the Northern Militarists without seeming to be in league with the foreign invaders. The capture of Peking marked the end of the Northern Punitive Expedition. In accordance with the revolutionary program of Dr. Sun, the period of military operations theoretically came to a close.

For the last year and a half the Nationalist leaders have been trying to consolidate their conquests and establish their power on a better basis than that of a vulgar military dictatorship. Recognizing the truth of the old saying that you can do anything with bayonets but sit on them, they have sought to follow the program laid down by Dr. Sun for strengthening the moral foundation of their power. For a time Chiang Kai-shek was the leader in this effort to sub-stitute pacific for military dictatorship in accordance with the program of Dr. Sun. He was one of the first to raise the cry "Back to the three principles of the people and the policies of Sun Yat-sen." But as time passed the opposition to his leadership became more and more intractable. Chiang Kai-shek fell into some of the errors of the early militarists and came to rely more and more upon military force and official violence for the maintenance of his power. Yet he has continued to respect the forms and proc-esses of government, established in the name of the Nationalist Party. He is a party "boss" as well as a military chieftain.

It is evident that the present government at Nanking, while nominally republican in form, like the parliamentary and soviet governments which preceded it, is in fact a dictatorship. This fact, how-ever, does not condemn it from the standpoint of Chinese Revolutionists, since the official theory of the Chinese Revolution, as formulated by Dr. Sun, calls for a dictatorship at this stage of the revolution. But the official theory calls for a pacific dictatorship, characterized by the predominance of educational over military activities; and as yet the Nanking Gov-ernment has been preoccupied with activities of the latter kind. It is too soon, perhaps, to know whether

Chiang Kai-shek is the man to transform the government from a military into a pacific dictatorship in accordance with the plans of Dr. Sun for the political reconstruction of China; but it is not too soon to attempt a provisional appraisal of Chiang Kai-shek's services to the Chinese Revolution.

In the first place, he is entitled to a large share of the credit for providing the revolutionary idea with the bayonets, which it needed in order to achieve success. As the head of the Whampoa military academy, he trained the officers who gave the revolutionary armies for the first time the indispensable combination of political reliability and military efficiency. In this work, he was greatly aided by General Galens and the other Russian and German military advisers, who were one of the principal fruits of the *entente cordiale* between Moscow and Canton. No doubt, too, the morale of the revolutionary armies was dependent in part upon the political agents and propagandists, who were trained in the political training institutes organized by Borodin and the other Communist political advisers at Canton; but Chiang Kai-shek was certainly the most capable and effective of the Chinese leaders produced by the Cantonese political-military machine, as he was also the most influential of its members.

Secondly, whatever may be his position in the government of the New China of the future, his name will go down in history as the principal leader of the so-called Northern Punitive Expedition, which in the space of two years, despite the greatest obstacles, overthrew the power of the old militarists at Peking and brought the whole of China under the Nationalist colors. The Nationalists, to be sure, were still far short of attaining their objectives. Their flag was flying over all the Chinese provinces, but the authority of their government had not followed the flag. In most provinces there had been a revolution of colors without much real change in the political practices of the militarists who actually held sway. The old militarists had been routed, but the unification of China was still more nominal than real. Nevertheless, the way had been opened for the reconstruction of the republic in accordance with the program of Sun Yat-sen, and in the military operations which had opened up the way, Chiang Kai-shek's name had led all the rest.

Thirdly, he is entitled to a generous portion of the credit for checking the spread of Communist influence in China in the spring of 1927. There is much discussion among Chinese Revolutionists as to whether the methods which Chiang Kai-shek adopted were the wisest. Many Revolutionists believed then, and still believe, that it would have been wiser to have respected the authority of the Nation-

alist Government at Hankow, and to have fought
the Communists within the Party, instead of setting
up a new government at Nanking and thereby
bringing about a schism in the revolutionary organization, which at the time almost wrecked the revolutionary movement and ever since has continued
to impair its strength. Those, who thought the Communist menace could have been averted without dis-
rupting the Party, cannot forgive Chiang Kai-shek
for his repudiation of the Hankow Government in
the spring of 1927, a government which, whatever
its faults of domestic policy, had the great merit in
the eyes of patriotic Chinese of asserting the rights
of China among the Powers with more vigor and
success than any other Chinese Government in
modern times.

Fourthly, Chiang Kai-shek is entitled to the credit
of vindicating Dr. Sun's political philosophy in the
face of the attack upon it by the Communists. It is
to his leadership that must largely be ascribed the
adoption of the organic law in the fall of 1928, which
is intended to prepare the way for the eventual
establishment of a democratic constitution such as
Dr. Sun advocated. Thus Chiang Kai-shek led the
revolutionary movement back into genuinely Chinese channels. If the political philosophy of Sun
Yat-sen is sound, the value of these services to China

will in the fullness of time undoubtedly appear to be very great. (Whether or not it is sound, is a question I shall discuss in a later chapter.)

Against these services must be offset some important disservices. In the first place, there is the disruption of the Nationalist Party, for which Chiang Kai-shek must take a large measure of the blame. Not only did he take the lead in the schism of 1927, but his management of the Third Party Congress, which met at Nanking in the spring of 1929, tended to widen the breach between the different factions of the Party. If the Nationalist movement is, as most patriotic Chinese believe, China's best hope for the regeneration of the state, the disruption of the Party has been a great misfortune. It has grievously impaired the moral authority of the new Nationalist Government, and without that moral authority, its claims to the allegiance of thinking and patriotic Chinese would be no better than that of the old militarists, whom the Nationalists overthrew.

Secondly, Chiang Kai-shek's disposition to rely more and more on military force and violence, not only has tended towards the establishment of a new militarism not easily distinguished from the old, but also this excessive reliance upon military force has interfered with the advancement of the social aims of the Revolution. Public revenues greatly needed for financing public improvements continue to be diverted into military channels, and the indispensable improvement of the living conditions of the people of China continues to be postponed to an indefinite future. Chiang Kai-shek's preoccupation with military activities leads him into the same error that proved so injurious to Yuan Shih-kai, namely, the failure to use the best men in the management of public affairs; and the personnel of the government at Nanking, though superior to that of any of the governments in modern times at Peking, falls far short of the standards which the Nationalist leaders had taught the people of China to expect.

Finally, Chiang Kai-shek's inability to suppress rebellion threatens the whole revolutionary movement with ruin. Unless he can restore the morale of the Nationalist Party, it is difficult to believe that he can stabilize his authority. It is evident that the military spirit is still the predominating influence in contemporary Chinese politics. The generals who continue to contend for mastery demonstrate by their contentiousness that the distinction between war and politics continues to be negligible, and that the military stage of the Revolution, which theoretically should have ended with the hoisting of the Nationalist flag over all China, has not yet been brought to an end. The stage of political tutelage, which according to the revolutionary philosophy of Sun Yat-sen should already have begun, remains still to be inaugurated in fact. The institutions appropriate for such a period have been established on paper, but they do not function as yet in accordance with the specifications of Dr. Sun's plans of reconstruction. There seems to be no ready and easy way of changing the personnel of the Nationalist Government except by fighting, and, until the supremacy of the civil authorities over the military can be definitely established, politics will continue to be distinguished with difficulty from civil war.

Nor is there any prospect that this result can be altered by any of the influences which have been heretofore considered in these lectures. Neither the spirit of democracy, nor that of Bolshevism, nor that of religion, appears strong enough to put the militarists in their place and establish law and order. The parliamentary system and the soviet system both have failed. There remain to be considered two other influences, however, which may be expected to help stabilize the New China, namely, the spirit of modern capitalism and that of modern science. These will be the subjects of the next two chapters.

V

T. V. SOONG AND THE SPIRIT OF CAPITALISM

IN the last chapter I discussed the military spirit in the Chinese Revolution, and tried to show how the effort to destroy the power of the old militarists and unify China, has bred a crop of new militarists, who have succeeded to the power, and to some extent also to the point of view, of the old, and have brought about a new division of China into spheres of influence, which render the government of the country from a single point not much more effective, now that the seat of government is located at Nanking, than it was formerly when located at Peking. The government of China continues to be government chiefly by military dictators; though military dictatorship, as I tried also to show in my last chapter, is ill-suited to the circumstances and traditions of China.

In the West, also, there has been much experience with military dictatorship in its various forms, and the persistent efforts to establish the supremacy of the civil authorities over the military have been a striking characteristic of modern history. In many

European countries these efforts have not yet achieved success. Where civilian control has been most successfully established, it has been brought about in part by matching the power of the purse against the power of the sword, through the organization of the commercial and industrial classes and their control of taxation and of appropriations. Thus statesmen in the more advanced Western countries have succeeded in putting their rivals, the generals, in a subordinate position. They have stabilized their governments and made the authority of civilian politicians prevail over that of the war lords.

The question rises in the minds of Westerners, who view the present confusion and disorder in China, whether the Chinese war lords also might not be put in their place by similar methods. Could not Chinese business men and capitalists assert themselves against the contentious militarists, and organize a government in which, through the control of the tax power, they could establish at least a pacific dictatorship instead of the heavy-handed military dictatorships, which now fill the country with their armies and destroy the tranquillity of the people? In short, could not modern capitalism, by asserting its strength, bring order out of the present confusion in China, and guide the revolution toward a successful end? This is the question which I wish to discuss now.

It is necessary to begin by considering the economic condition of China. China is predominantly an agricultural country. A great majority of the population live in the villages. There are, to be sure, many large cities and, if all the walled cities and seats of government in the administrative districts be included, the total number of cities would mount up toward two thousand. But the organization of industry in these cities is for the most part essentially medieval. Goods are produced in small shops under the eye of the master with the aid of a few apprentices and journeymen. The master himself is an artisan or craftsman who works with his own hands and belongs to the local guild, by means of which he and his fellow masters regulate the conditions of their work. The apprentices and journeymen look forward to becoming masters and guildsmen in their turn and taking their part in the control of industry. It is only in the larger cities, that a revolution in industry has already begun and the growth of modern capitalism has created a new force of political importance.

The available information concerning the growth of modern capitalism is far from satisfactory. The Peking Government formerly maintained a bureau of economic information, which published some interesting material on the development of factories and the volume of production of the principal factory industries. Significant investigations have been

made also by economists and sociologists connected
with missionary colleges, but systematic information
in the form of a national census remains unavailable.
The most comprehensive data relating to modern
capitalism in China, which I have seen, were in Moscow, but I had no means of checking up their reliability.

It is clear that factory industry developed slowly
prior to the World War and hardly at all outside the
large treaty ports. Since the War the development
has been more rapid. The most important of the factory industries is the cotton textile industry, which
has grown with special rapidity in Shanghai and
Hankow, though not confined to these cities. In the
North flour milling is the leading factory industry.
It has made remarkable progress in the cities of the
grain growing regions, notably in Harbin, Tientsin,
and Tsinanfu. One of the important consequences
of the growth of modern capitalism is the development of labor organizations. The organization of
labor seems to have begun in the transport industry,
particularly among the waterside workers in the
large treaty ports at the close of the World War. It
then spread rapidly among the factory workers,
whose conditions of employment, judged by Western standards, were very bad, especially in the factories under Chinese control. By 1922, when the
First National Labor Conference met at Canton,

there were some two hundred unions reported in twelve different cities, with a membership on paper of three or four hundred thousand workers. Later, when the Chinese Soviet Republic reached the climax of its power after the removal of its capital from Canton to Hankow, the number of organized workers greatly increased and the Chinese Federation of Labor claimed between two and three million members. But this is only a rough measure of the development of a modern wage-earning class and of the factory system of industry.

Modern capitalism in China is financial and commercial as well as industrial. In such centers as Shanghai, Hankow, and Tientsin, its development has reached large proportions, and the general chambers of commerce in those cities are probably the most powerful non-political organizations in all China. But modern capitalism still affects directly only a small proportion of the producing masses of the country. The present political significance of the capitalist class results chiefly from the strategic importance of the great cities which it dominates. But its prospects of future greatness are impressive. The industrial revolution has reached China, and if the kind of law and order which are most conducive to the progress of modern capitalism could be established there, it would undoubtedly proceed with unparalleled rapidity. A country with such a

great area, such immense undeveloped natural resources, and such an intelligent and industrious population, offers a potential field for the investment of
capital unrivaled in the world today.

The development of modern capitalism in China,
however, requires something more than a great store
of natural resources and an unrivaled body of workers. Modern capitalism in the West has reached such
a high pitch of development, that we accept it as
the normal system of industry and are scarcely conscious of the nature of its foundations. It is necessary to recognize, not only the material foundation
of modern capitalism, but also the indispensable
psychological foundation. The present capitalistic
system in the West presupposes certain legal forms of
business organization and practice, particularly, the
business corporation with a limited liability for its
debts, and also a corresponding development of the
moral ideas, which alone make such a form of organization practicable. What these moral ideas are, is
evident enough, when one surveys the history of
modern capitalism in the West. At the beginning, intelligent observers were unable to believe that the
business corporation would prove a serviceable form
of industrial organization, except within narrow
limits. In businesses of a routine character, involving
the employment of large amounts of capital, such
as banking, insurance, the construction and opera-

tion of canals and turnpikes, etc., early economists, like Adam Smith, believed that the business corporation would be a useful device for bringing the needed sums of money under unified direction; but they were convinced that in ordinary lines of business the sense of personal responsibility, which accompanies a strictly individualistic system of business organization, would be indispensable. Anticipating that, under the corporate form of organization, the personal responsibility of the individual owner would be supplanted by the vague and indefinite corporate responsibility of salaried officials, they feared that large corporations would fall into the hands of unscrupulous promoters and directors, who would exploit their control of other people's money for private ends. They feared, too, that majority stockholders would oppress minority stockholders and deprive them of their fair share of the profits of the common busines. They dreaded the development of graft on a great scale.

We now know that there was much ground for those apprehensions. The development of a corporate sense of responsibility on the part of the executives of big business has required a long time and has been accompanied by much bitter experience for minority stockholders and for investors generally. Gradually, however, the necessary morale for operating big business has been developed and we have today a sense of responsibility to investors and to the public on the part of the executives of our greatest corporations, which makes it possible to place in their hands the great power indispensable for the economical administration of large scale industry.

We have not yet developed in this country, most of our economists believe, the morale necessary for the successful administration of large-scale business operations by the government itself. Apart from some businesses of a comparatively simple routine character, such as the post office, our politicians and public officials, we are told, are not capable of operating great public utilities with the necessary economy and efficiency. State capitalism, they assert, is not for us. State socialism seems to such observers still more remote. The psychological foundation for democracy in industry seems to most of the economists of today as inadequate as that of large-scale corporate enterprise seemed to their predecessors of a century ago. We have gradually developed the morale for private capitalism, however, and we suspect that a people who have not yet developed the appropriate morale will find modern capitalism as difficult as state socialism presumably would be here under the existing conditions in the business and political world.

But these considerations raise an interesting question. If a people do not yet possess the morale appropriate for modern capitalism, might they not find some sort of socialistic régime as feasible as the kind of capitalism which we have developed in the West? Not militant Communism, such as some of the Russian political advisers sought to introduce in China, but a modified socialism, suited to the social capacity of the people? A new morale of some sort must be developed in China. Why not a socialistic morale, if that seems ultimately more promising, as well as a capitalistic morale?

In China there has always been a highly developed business morality, but it has been radically different from the current business morality of the West. A business man's first loyalty has been to his family, and Chinese capitalists have been slow to recognize the necessity for the development of new loyalties to stockholders and other investors outside the family. The morale necessary for the efficient management of the modern capitalistic system has been slow to emerge, and the strength of the competing claims of family loyalty make it apparently as difficult for Chinese business men to administer the affairs of a great corporation without excessive nepotism and graft, as it has been for Chinese politicians to assume the responsibilities of a modern government without excessive indulgence in the corresponding malpractices. Mr. Julean Arnold, the American commercial attache in China, relates an incident in his recent book, "Some Bigger Issues in China's Problem," which illustrates the nature of this psychological difficulty in the development of modern capitalism in China. "In changing from an individual to a corporate society," he writes, "we are confronted with a new conception of man's relations to his fellowmen. I recall an incident when, some years ago, a Chinese put up a considerable sum of money to meet the obligations of his brother, who had failed in a business project in which this man was not an interested party. I asked why he felt himself duty-bound to meet the obligations of his brother when he had no legal connection with the enterprise. He stated that the good name of his family was at stake and hence no other course of action was possible as long as he was in a financial position to give help. This same man was at the same time a director in a Chinese railway. Shares of this railway had been quite widely distributed among Chinese business men. Each of the directors took advantage of his place on the board to make money for himself at the expense of both the railway and the stockholders. In other words, where corporate had replaced individual responsibility, the man, who had been very conscientious in regard to his individual or family obligations, failed to show any appreciation for his responsibility as a trustee of the larger and less per-

sonal group. An obstacle of commanding significance," Mr. Arnold concludes, "to any efforts to
establish among the Chinese a proper conception of
the responsibilities of trusteeship in modern capitalistic industry is the nepotism which is associated with
the Chinese family system."

Thus the same old family system, which Borodin
and the other Bolshevist agents found such an obstacle to the success of Communism in China, lies
in the way also of the successful introduction of
modern capitalism. The latest Nationalist law codes
foster the substitution of legal concepts based upon
the Western principle of personal responsibility
rather than the Chinese principle of family responsibility. This is what the spirit of modern politics as
well as of modern capitalism requires. To convert
the Chinese from a family-conscious to a business-
corporation-conscious and state-conscious people
is an indispensable task of the Revolution. In a country as large and settled in its ways as China, it is an
educational enterprise of colossal magnitude.

Another prerequisite to the development of the
influence of modern capitalism in Chinese politics
is the growth of a greater interest in politics on the
part of Chinese business men. Chinese business men,
like other classes of Chinese, have from time imme-
morial regarded politics as the business of the politicians. They recognized that the classical scholars

were trained for politics, were compelled to demonstrate their fitness by rigorous examinations, and
were generously rewarded by success. Capitalists and
other business men, like farmers and laborers, had
their own affairs to attend to. As I have said before,
they felt no more personal responsibility for the conduct of affairs of state than American farmers and
laborers and ordinary business men feel for the management of the New York stock exchange. That is
the affair of the stock brokers and not of the public.
In America a stock broker buys his way into the exchange, while in China in the best days of the old
empire a scholar worked his way into the official
hierarchy, but the attitude of outsiders was much
the same toward both institutions. Insiders were
there to make their fortunes, and outsiders saw no
harm in that, as long as the institutions gave satisfactory service at reasonable rates. But modern government cannot be operated so easily. Outsiders as
well as insiders have their work to do, if it is to give
satisfaction. The business of government is a business
so affected with a public interest as to justify to the
Western mind the constant intervention of the public in the management of the business. The growth
of a similar attitude in China, on the part at least of
Chinese capitalists, is indispensable, if the power of
the purse is to become an efficient check on the power
of the sword.

Chinese capitalists, though reluctant to admit that the private business of the politicians has become a public business, have nevertheless been slowly awakening to the needs of the times. The most striking manifestation of the growing interest on the part of Chinese business men in the conduct of political affairs has been the series of great boycotts, directed now against one group of foreign traders and now against another, as the exigencies of Chinese politics have required. One of the earliest of these boycotts was that directed against American business men a quarter of a century ago on account of the American policy of excluding Orientals from the United States. In recent years the most effective boycotts have been directed against the English and the Japanese. After the Shanghai and Shameen incidents of 1925, boycotts against the British in China brought their trade to a standstill and did incalculable damage to British interests in the Far East. In Hong Kong, where the boycott was most effective, the government discontinued the distribution of commercial statistics, it was alleged, on grounds of economy; but empty counting houses and deserted wharves were mute witnesses of the extent of the damage. The Japanese have been the objects of destructive boycotts on several occasions, notably in connection with their occupation of Shantung under the Treaty of Versailles, and more recently at the time of their reoccupation of Shantung during the advance of the Nationalist armies in the spring of 1927 and again in 1928. These boycotts, though by no means one hundred percent effective, were impressive displays of the power of Chinese businessmen and of their growing interest in political affairs, and undoubtedly have been more effective weapons in dealing with aggressive imperialism than any directly in the hands of Chinese Governments.

Another significant expression of the growing tendency on the part of Chinese bankers and merchants, to regard political affairs as public affairs, was the organization of the Merchants Guard at Canton in 1924, to protect business interests against the threatened influence of Bolshevism. The crushing of this guard in the autumn of that year by Nationalist forces, led by officers trained in the methods of the Red army at the Whampoa military academy, established under Russian auspices, marks the turning point in the development of the modern Nationalist movement. It destroyed the power of the Chinese capitalists in Nationalist China until the spring of 1927, when the Chinese bankers and merchants in Shanghai entered politics with a fresh determination to check the spread of Communist influence in China, and financed the new Nationalist Government at Nanking. The lavish support, which the Chinese capitalists in Shanghai then gave to General

Chiang Kai-shek and his associates, was an important factor in checking the development of a Communist labor movement in Shanghai, and in forcing the elimination of Borodin and the Russian Communists from the Chinese revolutionary movement. Since the establishment of the Nationalist Government at Nanking, the Chinese bankers and merchants of Shanghai and vicinity have been its leading supporters, and have advanced enormous sums of money to sustain its credit. The Minister of Finance at Nanking, Mr. T. V. Soong, has been their special representative in the government, and a survey of his career throws much light on the influence of modern capitalism in the revolutionary movement and upon the prospects for the control of the sword by the purse.

T. V. Soong was born of a wealthy Christian Chinese family in Shanghai in 1891 and is, consequently, still under forty years of age. He studied in mission schools in Shanghai and then came to America to complete his education. He was enrolled for a time in Vanderbilt University at Nashville, Tennessee, and eventually came to Harvard, where he graduated in 1915. His special field at Harvard was economics and in the courses in that subject he took high rank. After his graduation he was employed for a time in a banking house in New York City, thereby supplementing his theoretical training with excellent

practical experience. Returning to China, he entered
upon a promising business career. But he could not
keep out of politics. His family had long been interested in the revolutionary movement, and eventually became allied by marriage with the most
prominent revolutionary leaders. His oldest sister
became the second wife of Dr. Sun, and was his constant companion and helpmate throughout the vicissitudes of his later career. After his death, she became
a member of the Central Executive Committee of
the Nationalist Party, and through her unswerving
loyalty to her husband's name and ideals acquired a
high position in the councils of the Party. A second
sister married Mr. H. H. Kung, a direct descendant
in the seventy-sixth generation of the great Confucius. Mr. Kung, now one of the cabinet-officers at
Nanking, was formerly an active worker in the
Y.M.C.A. and served as Chinese Secretary of the
"Y." at Tokyo and later at Taiyaanfu, the seat of
government of Yen Hsi-shan, the "model" governor
of Shansi province. A third sister became the wife of
Chiang Kai-shek. She has always taken a deep interest in revolutionary politics, and has exerted an
uncertain but quite possibly important influence
upon the policies of the Nanking Government. So-
cially ambitious mothers, regardless of race, will appreciate what it was to marry three daughters of
one family, respectively, to the father of the Rev-

olution, to the foremost living descendant of China's greatest man, and to the commanding general of the revolutionary armies. These matrimonial alliances opened the way for the rise of the House of Soong in revolutionary politics.

T. V. Soong was well equipped to take advantage of his extraordinary opportunity. To a high degree of native intelligence and buoyant energy, he added excellent training in modern finance and the best business experience that life in the Chinese treaty ports affords. Proceeding to Canton when the Nationalist Government established its seat there, he was appointed president of the state bank, and later Minister of Finance. Introducing the systematic fiscal practices which he had learned in America, he put a check on official fraud and corruption and caused the revenues of the republic to flow into the treasury in unprecedented abundance. His friends could apply to him the striking description which Webster once applied to Alexander Hamilton. "He struck the rock of the national resources and out gushed abundant streams of revenue. He touched the dead corpse of the national credit and it sprang to life." When T. V. Soong followed the Nationalist armies to Hankow, however, he was unable to repeat his success at Canton. The conditions at Hankow were different from those at Canton, and the Nationalist Government brought depression instead of

prosperity. But later at Nanking, where two years
ago he again resumed his role of Minister of Finance,
he succeeded in accomplishing the apparently impossible. He not only financed the Northern Expedition, but also secured the revenues necessary for
consolidating the Nationalist Government.

Under Mr. Soong's financial leadership the Chinese
capitalists of Shanghai and Ningpo continued, after
the defeat of the Northern Militarists, to back the
Nanking Government with their money. Mr. Soong
made the most strenuous efforts to unify the national finances, and to repeat on a nation-wide scale
the brilliant success he had formerly scored at Canton. In June, 1928, he convened a national economic
conference at Shanghai, which was the first general
conference of Chinese business men organized for
the purpose of making their influence felt in the conduct of public affairs. He laid down a program of
economy and efficiency in the financing of the Revolution which, if it could have been carried out,
would have gone far toward both unifying the government of the republic and establishing the supremacy of the civilian authorities over the militarists. But the Nationalist generals were reluctant to
disband their armies or to abandon the revenues
which made it possible for them to maintain such
armies. Mr. Soong could count only on the revenue
of four or five provinces for the support of the

Nanking Government, and the other provinces continued as before to support their local militarists at the expense of the national treasury.

The success of Mr. Soong's financial policy and the future of the capitalist influence in the Chinese Revolution depended upon the ability of the Nanking Government to reduce the armies and secure the revenues of the local militarists for general public purposes. In pursuance of this object, a military reorganization and disbandment conference was held at Nanking in January, 1929. The leading Nationalist generals were in attendance, and under pressure from Mr. Soong and the financial interests which he represented, a rational program for the limitation of armaments throughout Nationalist China was adopted. But before the program could be carried into effect, fighting broke out again and the Nationalist Government continued as before to give the first place to its military operations and to spend most of its money on arms and ammunition. In August, 1929, Mr. Soong brought together a so-called national disbandment enforcement conference in the hope that tangible progress in the limitation of armaments and release of revenues for pacific purpose might at last be made. But that conference, like its predecessors, failed to put a stop to the contention among the new militarists. Mr. Soong's high hopes for the balancing of revenues and expenditures and for the restoration of the public credit were again disappointed. He had brought financial experts from abroad, notably the mission under Professor Kemmerer of Princeton, the "financial doctor," as he has been called, and had spared no pains in order to introduce a sound financial system. Yet the results of his efforts continued to be unsatisfactory. The question arose, whether his financial backers, especially the great capitalists of Shanghai and Ningpo, could continue to support so expensive a government as that of Chiang Kai-shek at Nanking with such uncertain prospects of any return to themselves. After the failure of disbandment enforcement conference last August, Mr. Soong handed in his resignation, but Chiang Kai-shek, after a personal visit to the Chinese capitalists who were backing Mr. Soong, succeeded in persuading him to remain in office at Nanking. Now the two men seem likely to stand or fall together.

The progress which has been made toward establishing the power of the purse over that of the sword is illustrated by the fighting which has taken place in Nationalist China during the past year. After the defeat of the Northern Militarists and the capture of Peking in the spring of 1928, there was an end to the fighting for that year. But early in 1929 the dissensions among the war lords broke out again.

There were at least half-a-dozen notable military

operations in China during 1929, not including the
operations in Manchuria growing out of the dispute
between China and Soviet Russia over the Chinese
Eastern Railway. First, in the month of February
there was Chang Tsung-chang's filibustering expedition into Shantung, projected from his base in
the Japanese leased territory near Dairen and carried
out under cover of the Japanese occupation of the
Shantung railway zone. This discredited tyrant
found little support among those who formerly
suffered under his rule and was quickly put to flight,
when in May the Japanese evacuated the province.
Secondly, there was the rising of the so-called
Kwangsi group of militarists against the Nanking
Government, which broke out in Central China in
the month of March. After a sharp campaign Chiang
Kai-shek recovered Hankow in April, and the
Kwangsi leaders were driven out of Central China.
Resuming operations in the South in May, they were
again defeated and dispersed, though not until after
they had nearly captured Canton and seriously
threatened the authority of Nanking in that section of China. Thirdly, there was the clash of arms
between Feng Yu-hsiang and Chiang Kai-shek in
May. These were the first open hostilities between
these two great rivals, and a fight to a finish was
averted by a temporary armistice. Fourthly, there
was the dispute with Soviet Russia over the Manchu-

rian question, which incidentally involved Nanking in difficulties with Mukden as well as with Moscow. This nondescript war broke out in July and was not discontinued until December. Fifthly, there was the revolt of General Chang Fa-kwei, commander of one of the best of the Nationalist armies, who had greatly distinguished himself by his aggressive leadership during the first year of the Northern Punitive Expedition. In September he repudiated the authority of Nanking and led his army, which was then stationed in Central China, toward the south, with the intention of seizing Canton and establishing himself in power in that section of China. This affair culminated in a pitched battle outside Canton in December, where the Nanking forces, after a doubtful struggle, won a decisive victory. Sixthly, there was the second Feng-Chiang war, which broke out in October and, after gravely threatening the life of the Nanking Government, was ended by political rather than military manœuvres in November. Finally, there was the revolt of General Tang Sheng-chi, another of the principal Nationalist commanders, who turned against Nanking in December, but was quickly brought to terms, when the other military operations had been successfully concluded. Such in bare outline is the record of fighting in a year which the Nationalist Government had hoped to make noteworthy for an un-precedented peace and prosperity.

The record of the fighting during 1929 shows a doubtful struggle between sword and purse for as-cendancy in Chinese politics. But some provisional results may be noted. In the first place, it is evident that the unification of the country is still very im-perfect. The Nationalist flag floats over all China Proper and also Manchuria, but in a majority of the provinces the authority of the Nationalist Govern-ment at Nanking is more honored in the breach than in the observance. Secondly, the disorganization of the country seems somewhat less at the end of the year than at the beginning. In four of the seven mili-tary affairs, which have been noted, the insurgent leaders yielded to military force, and the lesson could not be without effect upon other militarists of simi-lar pretensions. Thirdly, the two wars, so-called, be-tween Feng and Chiang were not ended by military force but by financial settlements. Feng remains ap-parently as strong as ever, and if the Chinese capi-talists, who are supporting the Nanking Govern-ment, came off more cheaply than they could have hoped to do, if Chiang and Feng had fought to a finish, the result is the practical partition of the country into spheres of influence and the postpone-ment of effective unification. Fourthly, the postponement of effective unification is still more clearly the result of the operations in Manchuria. The relationship between Nanking and Mukden defies classification upon the principles of politics recognized generally in the West. Fifthly, the influence of Chinese capitalism in the Nationalist Government at Nanking seems to have increased and to be increasing. The tendency seems to be for that government to become less militaristic and more capitalistic. Sixthly, modern capitalism has become an undoubted force in the political reconstruction of China, which must be reckoned with in the future, along with the new militarists and the new politicians, that is, the leaders of the Nationalist Party.

It is evident further that the Chinese capitalistic interests have a difficult task ahead of them to establish the mastery of the purse over the sword, and that they cannot hope to accomplish the task by the same methods that have been successful in the West. In the West the rise of modern capitalism in politics has gone hand in hand with the development of representative government. It is through parliamentary or congressional institutions that the commercial and industrial classes of Western Europe and America have controlled the powers to tax and to appropriate the public money, upon which their political ascendency has depended. But in China the effort to introduce representative government in any of its typical Western forms has failed. Not only has the parliamentary republic failed, but also the much simpler form of representative government contemplated by the advocates of the soviet system. If the modern capitalist class in China is to exert a strong and potentially preponderant influence in Chinese politics some form of government must be found better suited to the conditions which prevail in China than any of those heretofore tried since the beginning of the Revolution. It is not enough that the modern capitalistic system should make progress in China. It is necessary also that the revolution in politics should take a form favorable to the growth of the influence of the capitalist class.

Any opinion concerning the prospects for greater influence on the part of capitalistic interests in the future course of the Chinese Revolution must depend in part upon the program of the Revolution with respect to modern capitalism as set forth in the writings of Sun Yat-sen. Dr. Sun was thoroughly convinced that the success of the Revolution depended upon a material as well as a spiritual reconstruction of China. He gave much thought to plans for the development of the natural resources of China and of the means of communication, and for the improvement of the conditions of its people. His plans were worked out for foreign governments and investors in his book, "The International Develop-

ment of China," written after the end of the World
War, when it seemed that foreign capital would
again be ready for investment in China. "Chinese
aspirations," he wrote, "can be realized only when
we understand that, to regenerate the state, we must
welcome the influx of foreign capital on the largest
possible scale, and also must attract foreign scientists
and trained experts. Then, in the course of a few
years, we shall develop our own powerful large scale
industry and shall accumulate technical and scientific knowledge." Thus, he believed, full development of the economic resources of China would be
possible, and only then would it be practicable to
complete the education of the people, so as to fit
them for the duties of citizenship in a democratic
republic.

But Dr. Sun did not believe it wise to encourage
the development of modern capitalism in China
without adopting proper safeguards to protect the
people against the abuses which had accompanied
the development of modern capitalism in the West.
With this thought in mind, he developed the third
of his famous three principles of the people—the so-
called principle of livelihood. This principle was
based upon the assumption that the needs of all
should be supplied as far as possible by the efforts of
all, and led him to a theory of government regula-
tion and control of the use of capital. Such a prin-

ciple might lead to one of the Utopian socialisms of a century ago, or to the more rigorous Marxism of the modern Communists, or even to the more moderate socialism favored by the independent labor parties of the West. In fact, Sun Yat-sen's social policy is identical with none of these. He deliberately rejected the word "socialism" on account of the many different meanings, which have been attached to it, and the quarrels, among those who use it, concerning its proper interpretation. "As a result," he declared, "the common people feel that there is nothing definite to follow in socialism." There is indeed no satisfactory word in English to describe the kind of social policy which Dr. Sun favored.

The great problem in Dr. Sun's eyes was how to secure the necessary capital from abroad without compromising the independence of China. He understood the implications of the connection between the material development of a country and its political stability. Knowing the matchless opportunities for the profitable investment of capital in China, he had no doubt that it would be forthcoming, in abundance, if the national credit was satisfactory to the foreign investor. Capital, proverbially timid, would be disposed, he perceived, to wait for the rehabilitation of the Chinese political system. If the national credit could not be revived without the rehabilitation of the state, neither could the state be efficiently unified and its government strengthened without the material reconstruction which must wait upon an improved national credit. It was an awkward dilemma. When Dr. Sun first formulated his plans, it required courage for a Chinese to insist that the political and industrial revolutions should go hand in hand. Foreign capitalists, as well as Chinese mandarins of the old school, were reluctant to believe that the obstacles to the material development of the country were so formidable. But time has shown that Dr. Sun was right.

The radical innovation in Sun Yat-sen's program for the international development of China is his insistence upon the participation of the state in the control of the capital. In other countries, where there has been a great demand for foreign capital, the problem of the government has been to furnish acceptable security for the payment of the interest and the eventual repayment of the principal. The obligations imposed upon debtor states in the interest of their creditors have done their part to give modern imperialism its unpopularity in the financially dependent countries. Dr. Sun believed that the best security for a foreign loan is a strong popular government, that where such security exists no other is necessary or proper, and that the inconsiderate grant of improper security impedes the creation of security of the right kind. Hence, his opposition to concessions likely to get out of control by the people of China or their representatives. His was a theory of public credit which may properly be described as anti-imperialistic but not as anti-capitalistic. After his death the prevalent suspicion of uncontrolled economic imperialism among his followers was exploited by the agents of Russian Communism to give the Chinese Revolution an anti-capitalistic and anti-foreign bias radically different from its original anti-imperialistic tendency. The Western Powers won their first encounter with Communism on Chinese soil, but they cannot expect to enjoy the fruits of their victory without coming to terms with the Revolutionists who have revived Dr. Sun's original principles. Adherents of modern capitalism in the West seek to justify it on the ground that it produces capital, when and where it is needed, in greater abundance and at less cost than any other economic system. It is necessary that the capitalistic system be justified in China by its works, or the struggle with Communism will blaze up again.

This is the problem which Chinese capitalists must solve, if they are to succeed in their endeavor to control the power of the sword by that of the purse. First, they have to put their own house in order by demonstrating their ability to conduct modern business on a great scale with a due regard for the interests of their stockholders and other investors, and of the

employees. They have to remember that the capitalistic system cannot be justified alone by the profits
secured by the insiders. It must also advance the interests of the masses of the people. No government,
least of all a capitalistic one, can become or remain
popular, unless it brings about some tangible better-
ment in the lives of the common people. It is not possible for the Nanking Government to ignore their
claims and maintain its character as a revolutionary
government, but it is possible to argue that for the
present the wisest method of improving the condition of the people is to promote an industrial rather
than further political revolution by encouraging the
introduction of machinery, the development of factories, and the rise of modern capitalism. An industrial revolution would absorb the surplus soldiers,
give unprecedented employment to labor, and mul-
tiply the fruits of the toil of the peasants. It was the
lack of capital, which caused Dr. Sun the most concern when he was planning the reconstruction of
China after the first revolution. It was the lack of
capitalists and consequently of a proletariat, which
embarrassed Borodin and, he believed, wrecked the
prospects of the Chinese Soviet Republic. It is still
the lack of capital and capitalists that hampers the
government at Nanking in the execution of its plans
for the improvement of the condition of the people.
It is the weakness of the Chinese capitalist class,

which makes it difficult for the revolutionary forces to put the new militarists more promptly in their places. The establishment of modern capitalism, the stabilization of the revolutionary government, and the improvement of the condition of the people are all bound up together.

Dr. Sun's vision of the New China was one in which the power of the state was to be used to the end that the needs of all should be supplied by the efforts of all. This vision requires that the New China shall be not only a political but also an industrial democracy. The period of constitutional government, in which the Revolution, according to Dr. Sun's program of reconstruction, will culminate, will be one in which there will be constitutional government in industry as well as in politics. The principal public officials in such a state will be the leaders of a civil service for business as well as for government. In such a state the interests of the dominant classes in capitalistic industry and in government would be more closely bound up together than heretofore, and in such a union there would be greater strength for the governing class as a whole. But politicians, who are also captains of industry, will abuse their power, unless subjected to moral restraints no less efficacious than those which make modern capitalism a tolerable and serviceable régime in the capitalistic states of the West. To the Occidental mind the development of the necessary political and social morale seems the most visionary of all the Chinese revolutionary visions. But to the Chinese, with their highly developed social capacity, the cultivation of the morale appropriate for state capitalism seems to offer no greater difficulties than that of the morale appropriate for private capitalism. If the revolutionary spirit is capable of the latter achievement, it should, in their opinion, be equally capable of the former.

It is this vision of an enterprising and high-powered government, and ultimately of an industrial as well as a political democracy, which makes Dr. Sun's program for the regeneration of China such a fascinating subject of study. My next chapter will be devoted to a further inquiry into this subject.

VI

C. T. WANG AND THE SPIRIT
OF SCIENCE

NOTHING is more surprising to those who approach the study of politics in a scientific
frame of mind than to couple the name of a practical
politician with the spirit of modern science. C. T.
Wang, the present Minister of Foreign Affairs at
Nanking, is surely no scientist in the ordinary sense
of the word, and but for his political position would
certainly not be mentioned in this chapter. Why,
one may ask, do I not cite one of the real scientists,
of whom there are not a few in contemporary China,
whose work has brought fresh distinction to Chinese
scholarship and aided in advancing the mastery of
man over nature in that country? Why do I not
mention Dr. V. K. Ting, for instance, whose work at
the head of the Chinese Geological Survey attests his
scientific competence, or Dr. J. H. Liu, formerly
superintendent of the hospital at the Peking Union
Medical College and recently Minister of Public
Health at Nanking? Dr. Liu is a graduate of Harvard College and also of the Harvard Medical School,
and it would have been a special pleasure for me to

have summoned such a man, to bear witness to the
interest of Chinese in the advancement of science and
to their ability to make it serve the needs of man-
kind. Or I might have mentioned Foreign Minister
Wang's brother, who is an eminent civil engineer, or
his nephew, a distinguished member of the faculty of
the Peking Union Medical College. But he himself
makes no pretensions to eminence in any branch of
natural science, and at the moment is nothing, if
not a practical politician.

When I first began the preparation of these chapters several months ago, few observers of Chinese
politics believed that Foreign Minister Wang would
continue for long to be a successful, even if practical,
politician. Amidst all the confusion and disorder that
has prevailed in China during recent months, it
seemed unlikely that the present Nanking Government could last out the year, and almost impossible
that the Minister of Foreign Affairs should be able
to retain his position. The discomfiture of Chinese
diplomacy in the dispute with Soviet Russia over
Manchuria, to say nothing of domestic embarrass-
ments, seemed to spell his doom. In fact he has ten-
dered his resignation at least once, and, I suppose,
his term of office may come to an end any day. But
if he had been displaced, his successor would probably have served my purpose equally well; for he
would have been succeeded by a man of similar

training and experience, and my purpose is to discuss Chinese political science, not the natural science which Westerners generally think of, when science is mentioned. The real subject of this chapter, as far as it is personified by any man, is none of China's living scientists, natural or political, but Sun Yatsen himself, a revolutionary leader not only, but also the founder of the New China's science of politics.

But I am glad to have an opportunity to sketch the career of C. T. Wang. I am glad, first, because it was in conversation with him at the headquarters of the Christian General in Central China on the eve of the spring campaign in 1928 that I gained a better understanding of the spirit of Chinese political philosophy, and, secondly, because his career affords an interesting illustration of the kind of training and experience that has made Young China what it is today.

C. T. Wang was born in Ningpo, one of the original treaty-ports on the Chinese coast, forty-eight years ago. His father was an Episcopal clergyman, and brought up his numerous family in the religion and the science of the West. C. T. Wang completed his education at Yale, where he graduated in 1910, one of the leading scholars of his class. During his years as an undergraduate at Yale, he was active in the religious work of the College, organizing and leading a bible class of Chinese students and serving also as traveling secretary in charge of the religious work among all the Chinese students in America. In addition, he served as president of the Chinese Students' Alliance. Returning to China, he went to work for the Y.M.C.A., and eventually became the general secretary of the Chinese "Y.," the most important position in the missionary world then open to a Chinese. Plunging into revolutionary politics along with his missionary activities, he took part in the outbreak of the revolution at Hankow in the Fall of 1911, and helped to draft the first provisional constitution of China. Elected to the first parliament, he became one of the leaders of the Nationalist Party and shared in the vicissitudes which subsequently fell to the lot of Dr. Sun's closest followers. In 1919 he went to Paris as the special representative of the revolutionary government at Canton, and was foremost in urging the Chinese delegates to withhold their signatures from the treaty of Versailles on account of the cession of German rights in Shantung to the Japanese. In 1922, following the Washington Conference, he was entrusted with the negotiations with Japan for the return of the Shantung railroad to China and carried them to a successful conclusion. He also conducted the negotiations with the Russians in 1924, which led to the recognition of the Soviet Union by China and to the present arrangement governing the Chinese

Eastern Railway in Manchuria. After the coup d'état in the fall of 1924, C. T. Wang became one of the leaders in the government established by Marshal Feng and Chang Tso-lin at Peking, and after these two quarreled, Wang, who stood with the Christian General, was forced to flee. Taking refuge in Shanghai, he had no part in the soviet governments at Canton and Hankow, but supported the moderate Nationalist Government, which was organized by Chiang Kai-shek at Nanking in the spring of 1927, and took office in 1928 as Minister of Foreign Affairs. It is too soon to pass judgment on his diplomacy, and in any case any consideration of the foreign policy of Nanking lies outside the field of these chapters. It is enough to point out that, to an excellent general education, judged by American standards, C. T. Wang adds extraordinary practical experience with affairs of state. Though still a young man, as foreign ministers go, he would appear to be exceptionally well qualified to interpret the spirit of modern Chinese political science.

The present age in China has often been compared by Western writers to the age of the Renaissance in Western Europe.[1] The movement in Western Europe known as the Renaissance was, as its name indicates, a rebirth. It was a rebirth of an old, long forgotten

[1] See the interesting article by Dr. Stephen P. Duggan, entitled, "Factors in the Chinese Situation," in the *Political Science Quarterly*, vol. XLIV, pp. 379–396 (September, 1929).

way of looking at life, the way of ancient Greece and Rome. That way of looking at life centered man's education upon himself and his daily life, his art, his literature and his philosophy. It had been eventually succeeded in the Western World by the Christian way of looking at life, and men were taught to despise the things of this world. To a greater extent than in the great days of classical antiquity they were preoccupied with other-worldly matters. The Renaissance caused men to turn once more with avidity to the cultivation of the senses, the emotions, and the intellect. It revolutionized the culture of Western peoples and eventually made progress rather than perfection, as in the Middle Ages, the ideal of modern times.

The China of today has likewise been invaded by a new learning. The Chinese are having their renaissance, but it is very different from that of the West. Instead of a revival of ancient learning, their renaissance has meant a discarding of ancient learning and a search for new inspiration through the culture of the West. But the novel element in modern Western culture is neither its art, its literature or its philosophy, but its science. Western science is based upon the habit of experiment, and that habit in turn presupposes liberty, liberty of thought and liberty of enterprise. Science refuses to accept anything on authority. It has no reverence for tradition. Investigation to get the facts and determination to be guided by them is its chief characteristic.

The spirit of modern science is obviously incompatible with the traditional Chinese culture. This culture was based upon authority and sanctified by the worship of ancestors. The opinions of the ancestors constituted the chief, indeed almost the sole, material of education. The correct understanding of those views was the primary aim of the old learning. Success in such learning was rewarded by admission to the hierarchy of scholars, which governed the empire. To the old-fashioned Chinese scholar the long continued existence of his civilization, while so many other civilizations rose and fell, was evidence enough of the wisdom of the ancestors.

This attitude is strikingly reflected in the mandate, which the great Manchu emperor, Chien Lung, sent to George III by Lord Macartnay, the head of a British diplomatic mission sent out to the Far East in 1793. "You, O King [that is, George III] live beyond the confines of many seas. Nevertheless, impelled by your humble desire to partake of the benefits of our civilization, you have dispatched a mission respectfully bearing your memorial. . . . I have perused your memorial. The earnest terms in which it is couched reveal a respectful humility on your part,

which is highly praiseworthy. . . . As to your en-
treaty to send one of your nationals to be accredited
to my celestial court and to be in control of your
country's trade with China, this request is contrary
to all usage of my dynasty and cannot possibly be
entertained. . . . If you assert that your reverence
for our celestial dynasty fills you with a desire to
acquire our civilization, our ceremonies and code of
law differ so completely from your own, that even
if your envoy were able to acquire the rudiments of
our civilization, you could not possibly transplant
our manners and customs to your alien soil. . . .
Swaying the wide world, I have but one aim in view,
namely, to maintain a perfect government and to
fulfill the duties of the state. Strange and costly objects do not interest me. If I have commanded that
the tribute offerings sent by you, O King, are to be
accepted, this was solely in consideration of the spirit
which prompted you to dispatch them from afar.
Our dynasty's majestic virtue has penetrated into
other countries and kings of all nations have offered
their costly tribute by land and sea. As your am-
bassador can see for himself, we possess all things.
I set no value on objects strange or ingenious, and
have no use for your country's manufactures."

That proud reply to the overtures of the younger
Pitt reveals well enough the spirit of the old régime
in China. But whatever one may think of the com-

parative merits of the Chinese culture and that of the West in former times, there could be no doubt of the superiority, at least in strength, of those who were the masters of the new science, and at last it was no longer possible for the more thoughtful Chinese to deny the necessity of accepting a part at least of the new Western learning. The Japanese led the way in the study of Western civilization and were quick to perceive wherein lay its superior strength. They recognized that the foundation of Western force was science. The physical sciences made Westerners strong in industry, and their applications to warfare made them strong in international relations. The Japanese, therefore, imported teachers of science, and her spectacular victories in the wars with China and with Russia attested the wisdom of her rulers and rang down the curtain upon the old order in Far Eastern politics.

The reception of Western science in China was bound to shake the very foundation of Chinese civilization. Western science exalts the individual and in China the individual has counted for little. The Chinese classics taught that the whole social system is built upon the family, and the individual has scarcely any rights outside the family, except as a member of a trade guild or some other kind of fraternity. The reception of modern science means the breaking up of the old social and industrial system. The small shops of the guildsmen must give way to modern factories, and family loyalty, as pointed out in the last chapter, must give way to larger loyalties, above all, loyalties to the modern business corporation and to the modern state. This is not the time to discuss the effect of Western applied science upon the organization of industry and the conduct of life in general. I must content myself with presenting to you a few reflections concerning the reception of Western political science in China and its effects upon Chinese politics.

Government in imperial China was an art rather than a science. Indeed, in the eyes of the old Chinese classical scholars, the real rulers of the country, government was a fine art, the finest of the fine arts. Politics was a branch of ethics and the concept of the statesman was identified in principle with that of the gentleman and scholar. The Western view is, that government should be a science, and the training of statesmen pays less attention to etiquette and ceremonies and the observance of ancient rites than to accounting and statistics and applied psychology, particularly the modern technique for sustaining the power of rulers by the consent of the governed. Intelligent Chinese, however, upon analyzing the culture of the West, have become convinced that the West has been much less successful in the application of scientific methods to problems of government than to those of industry and commerce.

Sun Yat-sen, the father of the Chinese Revolution, discusses in a most interesting way in one of his books the comparative state of the natural and the social sciences in the West. In the natural sciences, he pointed out, the West has made amazing progress and man's command of nature has been enormously increased. Through the development of mechanical power not only rich men but also average men have secured the equivalent of the services of a multitude of slaves. The average citizen, therefore, in the modern state, has the independence and leisure, which only the rich possessed in former times. But while such great improvements have been made in the natural sciences and in their applications to the problems of life, there has been, he thought, no corresponding advance in political science.

On the contrary, as he saw it, the science of government has lagged far behind the other sciences. Westerners, Dr. Sun observed, still read Plato's *Republic* with interest and profit. They still find much to learn from the study of Aristotle's *Politics*, though no Westerner would turn to Aristotle's writings on natural science for any purpose but the gratification of idle curiosity. But despite the failure of the West to make any such remarkable discoveries in political science as in natural science, Dr. Sun was as hopeful for the improvement of the practical art of government by the methods of modern science, that is, by the systematic and purposeful study of political structure and political processes, as of improvement in other aspects of life by similar methods. If it were possible, he argued, to increase the power of the state, as mechanical power available for the service of man has been increased, and still keep this high-developed political power under popular control, the capacity of such a powerful state to enrich the life of the people would outstrip the imagination. In the West, he thought, people seemed to fear, that great political power would get out of control and be used for their oppression. Hence they preferred old-fashioned and comparatively weak forms of government to the powerful political machines which they might possess, if they dared to build them. Government, Dr. Sun said, is a "kind of invisible machine." Keeping to this figure of speech, he continued: "Visible machinery is built upon the laws of physics, while the invisible machinery of government is built upon the laws of psychology. Discoveries have been made in the field of physics for several hundred years, but the science of psychology only began twenty to thirty years ago, and is not yet far advanced.—Hence this difference," Dr. Sun argued. "In ways of controlling physical ob-

jects and things we should learn from the West, but
in ways of controlling men we should not learn only
from the West. The West long ago thought through
the principles and worked out the methods of physical control so we can wholly follow Western material civilization. . . . But the West has not yet
thought through its principles of government and
its methods of government have not yet been
fundamentally worked out. So China today, when
putting democracy into operation and reform-
ing its government, cannot simply follow the West.
We must think out a radically new method."

This quotation brings out the spirit of the revolutionary political science which Dr. Sun's followers
are teaching to the people of China. Occupying the
first place in this new science of politics is the theory
of revolution itself. Dr. Sun's theory of revolution
was embodied in his famous aphorism: "Understanding is difficult, action easy." Most revolutionists, he
had discovered, held precisely the contrary opinion.
They believed that it was action that was difficult,
whereas understanding was easy. In his writings he
was at great pains to controvert this notion. He cites
numerous examples of the truth that, though some
first learn to understand and thus know how to act,
a greater number without understanding can also
act. For instance, few people understand the process
of nutrition nor many the principles of dietetics, but

all can ordinarily choose their food so as to sustain life. Again, few persons could devise a serviceable standard of value and medium of exchange, nor do many understand the theory of money, but everybody can use it. Likewise, Dr. Sun believed, the coming of democracy to China need not wait until the science of government is universally understood, or even until there is general knowledge of the principal features of a democratic constitution. For the masses of the people, he believed, it is enough to desire that kind of government, and to be willing to do what is required of them in order that it may be maintained. In the first place, the political agitator, and subsequently the educator, will try to spread among the people those attitudes of mind which make them suitable material for democratic states. They will cultivate the disposition to demand popular government and to imitate the behavior of those who will show them the way to operate such a government. Dr. Sun, in his writings, lays great stress on three characteristics of good citizenship in a democracy; namely, wisdom, courage, and love of one's fellowmen. But not all these qualities seem to him equally necessary for all classes of people. All the people certainly need the third, love of their fellowmen. Ordinarily, politicians need the second as well, but only the architects of states or state planners, as we might call those who reform constitutions, are most in need of the first.

And so Dr. Sun's theory of revolution distinguishes between three successive stages of the revolutionary process. The first is the overthrow of the old order and the establishment of the revolutionists in power. This has to be accomplished by military force and violence. During this stage of the revolution, there will necessarily be a military government, and the people will be the instruments rather than the associates of the revolutionary leaders. The second stage should be devoted to the training of the people in the rights and duties of citizenship, and to the training of the leaders in the practical art of politics. During this stage of the revolution the government would continue to be in the hands of the revolutionary leaders without direct control by the people. This is what the Chinese Revolutionists call the period of political tutelage, and in theory it is the stage which the Revolution has now reached. The final stage of the revolutionary process would be marked by the establishment of a democratic constitution. The revolutionary leaders would become constitutional rulers, and the people would exercise the rights necessary for the maintenance of their sovereignty. But the period of constitutional government would not necessarily be inaugurated everywhere at the same time. When any province should be reduced to order, according to Dr. Sun's instructions, military government would give way to political tutelage in that province. When the people of any administrative district within such a province should become fit for self-government, tutelage would give way to popular government in that district. When all the districts in a province should enjoy popular government, a democratic constitution would be ordained for the province as a whole. When tutelage shall have yielded to a constitutional system in a majority of the provinces, China will be ripe, according to Dr. Sun's theory of revolution, for a national constitutional government. Then a national constitution will be established. This is the program which Dr. Sun has outlined for the conduct of the Revolution.

Sun Yat-sen's second contribution to modern political theory is his theory of education. He believed that the educational system of a state is the essence of its constitution, and that the chief object of education in a rightly organized state is training for public life. To the Chinese this is a thoroughly conservative theory of education. It is the theory set forth in their ancient classics. To inculcate it was one of the principal duties of the mandarins in the classical empire. The main purpose of the ceremonies in the temples of Confucius was to emphasize its importance. Dr. Sun was clinging to the best traditions of China, when he repeated the familiar exhortation from the Confucian text-book, "The Great Learning." "Search into the nature of things," the Sage had said, "extend the boundaries of knowledge, make the purpose sincere, regulate the mind, cultivate personal virtue, rule the family, govern the state, pacify the world." Dr. Sun agreed with Confucius that this was the right order in which to proceed. Effective training for public life should begin with the diffusion of knowledge and the development of character, and should not end until all the world should find peace. So he praised the ancient Chinese morality like any mandarin of the old school.

But from this theory of education, Dr. Sun's followers drew quite different practical conclusions from those drawn by the classical scholars of old China. Believing, as the old scholars did, that men were equal by nature in the sense that all men are naturally good, they deemed them very unequal in strength, intelligence and political capacity. Such natural inequalities of men were the justification of the peculiar institutions of the old empire. Those who could not pass the examinations for admission into the hierarchy of politicians were, in their opinion, manifestly unfit for participation in affairs of state. They were supposed to mind their own business and leave the conduct of affairs of state to statesmen. When democratic reformers like Dr. Sun began to argue that the conduct of public affairs should cease to be the private business of the ruling class and should become a public business, they were told that it would be impossible to transform China into a modern state, until the whole Chinese people had received a modern education. "You imagine," the skeptics cried, "that China can immediately in a single jump become a strong and vigorous state qualified for a place among the great Powers. But it will take years for the diffusion of universal education among the hundreds of millions of Chinese, and meanwhile the state will be ruined by the admission of the unfit to positions of authority and power."

Dr. Sun was in partial agreement with the critics of democracy. Though he had faith in the political capacity of the Chinese people, he did not believe that all possessed equal capacity. As they began to reform the government and to apply democracy, a part, he thought, should be given to every man, but the part should be suited to the man's capacities. "We must realize," he said, "that political democracy is not given to us by nature. It is created by human effort. We must create democracy and then give it to the people, not wait to give it until the people fight for it." By the expression "create democracy," Dr. Sun meant to devise the plan for a democratic state, and by giving it to the people, he meant teaching the people how to operate the state according to the plan. The people need not wait for democracy, he thought, until they have learned to act like democrats. Those who wish to become swimmers do not stay out of the water until they know how to swim.

Dr. Sun's chief contribution to the theory of political education is his distinction between education for citizenship and education for statesmanship. In Western democracies this distinction is not recognized, since democracy is understood to mean that everyone may rule and be ruled in turn. But the West, he believed, had not succeeded in solving the problem of democracy. The science of government in the West had lagged far behind the other sciences. He concluded that, while all citizens should be educated for citizenship, only those who are naturally fit should be educated for statesmanship.

The practical effect of this theory of political education was the revival of interest among Chinese Revolutionists in their ancient political ideas and in the political institutions which those ideas supported. Rejecting the conventional Western doctrines of natural and equal rights, Dr. Sun insisted upon the difference between the organization of the state and the administration of the government. The function of the people in a democracy, he reiterated, was to control the government and that of the most capable men to operate it. There is nothing new, perhaps, in Dr. Sun's distinction between the exercise of sovereign power and the employment of political ability. Western democracies have rarely ventured to practice what the more radical democratic theorists have preached. Everywhere we now find efforts to separate politics from the technical administration of public affairs, and the study of the proper relations between the permanent administrative officers and the representatives of the people has an important place in the science of popular government. The service of Sun Yat-sen was to give new emphasis to an old truth, which the Chinese discovered long ago, and to create new respect for old institutions, which the Chinese could more easily adapt to modern conditions than replace by strange institutions from abroad. This was a service of inestimable value to the Chinese Revolution.

Dr. Sun's theory of political education introduces the third of his major contributions to modern political science, namely, his theory of government. His chief contribution to the theory of government is his emphasis upon the distinction between sovereignty and political ability. Western democratic theory holds that all should be able to rule and to be ruled alike. It is based upon the assumption that all men are created equal and are endowed by their creator with certain inalienable rights. Sovereignty, that is the control of public policy, argued Dr. Sun, should be vested in all the people, but the public offices should be filled by those only who are able efficiently to perform their duties. The value of this distinction, he pointed out, depends upon the adoption by the people of the appropriate attitude toward the business of government. It may be like the attitude of owners of a private business, who entrust others with the actual conduct of affairs. The owners engage men of superior ability to operate the enterprise, while they retain the control of sovereignty. In the factory, Dr. Sun adds, only the general manager gives orders. The stockholders simply have supervision over him. The people of a republic are stockholders in the state and should look upon the government as a body of experts in statesmanship. With such an attitude, Dr. Sun argued, public as well as private business can be well administered. But in none of the democratic states of the West, he thought, do the people have such an attitude toward government, and hence they cannot make effective use of competent men to direct the government. As a result, the men in public life seemed to him generally incompetent, and democratic government seemed to be the least satisfactory of the products of the machine age in the West.

Dr. Sun thought that democratic states had pro-
gressed less rapidly than autocratic states like Japan.
Japan, he said, has been modernized for only a few
decades, but is now wealthy and powerful. People
in Western democracies know that they ought to
use experts in government as well as in private business, but they have not succeeded in doing so.
Wealthy owners of automobiles employ expert
chauffeurs to keep their cars in good running order
and to drive them. The chauffeur can do this better
than the owner, though the owner retains the control and directs the movements of his car. So it
should be, Dr. Sun argued, in government. Once the
people have the correct attitude toward their public
servants, democratic states can be well governed. In
other words, it should not be necessary to sacrifice
the advantages of aristocracy in order to enjoy the
blessings of democracy.

Dr. Sun's plan of government was based upon this
distinction between sovereignty and ability. The
government of the state, he insisted, should be built
upon the rights of the people, but the administration
of public affairs should be entrusted only to experts.
The rights of the people, which in his opinion were
necessary for maintaining their due control over the
government, were four in number. These were the
direct election and recall of public officers and direct
legislation by means of the so-called popular initia-

tive and referendum. With these four powers he believed the people could control directly the government of their state. It would then be safe to con-
struct a high-powered, strong government, broad in
scope and capable of accomplishing great things. If a
powerful government should be installed in the
largest state in the world, Dr. Sun exclaimed, would
not that state outstrip all others? Would not that
government be unequalled under heaven? Here was
a project which made a strong appeal to the imaginations of patriotic Chinese.

Such was the reasoning upon which Dr. Sun proposed his plan for the so-called Five Power Constitution. This plan is based upon the Western doctrine
of the separation of powers. But it is worked out in
such a way as to combine with Western principles of
government such of the ancient Chinese principles
as seemed to Dr. Sun applicable to the new age. Besides the usual three departments of government,
recommended by Montesquieu and sanctified in the
Constitution of the United States, there are two
others, the examination department and the super-
visory department or censorate. No one was to be
deemed qualified for a place in the executive or even
in the legislative department, unless his competence
was first attested by the examiners, and no one was to
remain in any public office, if found to be unfit by
the censors. Examiners and censors are to be as inde-

pendent of one another and of the other departments of government as judges are of executives and
legislators under the best Western constitutions. The
plan called for a combination of the best features of
the constitution of the old scholastic empire with
what Dr. Sun believed to be best also in the constitutions of the West. "Such a government," he declared in a final burst of enthusiasm, "will be the
most complete and the finest in the world, and a
state with such a government will have indeed a
government of the people, by the people, and for the
people."

Dr. Sun's choice of terms suggests that he was
familiar with Abraham Lincoln's Gettysburg ad-
dress. In fact his famous "three principles of the
people" were largely inspired by Lincoln's conception of democracy. A government of the people
meant to Dr. Sun a government based upon the
principle of national independence. A government
by the people meant to him one based upon the
principle of popular sovereignty. A government
for the people meant one designed to promote the
general welfare, or, as he put it, based upon the
principle of popular livelihood. These were his three
principles of the people. Upon these principles he
built his revolutionary platform, consisting of three
planks, nationalism, democracy, and, what for lack
of a better name we may call, socialism. His idea of

socialism I have discussed in a previous lecture. His idea of nationalism is the cornerstone of the present foreign policy of the Nanking Government. In these chapters I have no time to consider the international relations of China. I can only hope to give you some idea of the program of domestic political reconstruction, which Dr. Sun has bequeathed to the present leaders of the Chinese Revolution.

Democracy, as Dr. Sun understood it, is the characteristic of a state, the government of which rests upon the expressed consent of the people who constitute it. But he was aware that Chinese democracy could not blindly follow in the path trod by the democrats of the West. He recognized that in China democratic institutions must be built upon the foundations which the age that is past has left to the age that is about to come. This recognition of the necessity of reconciling the political ideas of the West with the political traditions of China, if the work of the Revolution is to endure, is perhaps the greatest of Dr. Sun's services to the people of China.

The leaders of the Chinese Revolution have been slow to understand and to appreciate Dr. Sun's political philosophy. At first they thought it would be easy to imitate the political institutions of the West, as easy perhaps as to imitate the machinery and mechanical processes of the West. So Dr. Sun's associates, in the first flush of victory over the Manchus eighteen years ago, set up the institutions of a parliamentary republic. It took years of bitter experience with unregenerated mandarins and hostile militarists before the attempt to establish a parliamentary republic was abandoned as unsuited to China. There was a similar experience with the institutions of the soviet republic. More successful certainly than the parliamentary republic, the soviet republic nevertheless proved also all-suited to Chinese habits of mind and modes of political behavior. Now at last the Chinese have begun to appraise at more nearly their true value Dr. Sun's theories of revolution, of education, and of government. They are, again, exploring the foundations of the old political system, in order to discover how much may be utilized in building up the new, and they are trying, in accordance with his advice, to reconcile what is still serviceable in their ancient political system with what is most adaptable in the political systems of the West.

This is the real significance of the political experiment begun at Nanking a little over a year ago. The organic law of October 10, 1928, introduced in the central government of the Chinese Republic some of the features of the Five Power Constitution, which Dr. Sun recommended for the final period of constitutional government. At the same time, also in accordance with his advice, the revolutionary leaders began to reorganize the local governments in those parts of the country under their control. Recognizing at last that the political reconstruction of China is a task in which statesmen must begin at the bottom and gradually work up, they are laying the foundation for the new China deep and broad.

Such a work of political reconstruction will necessarily take a long time. It is idle to expect that the present dictatorship of the revolutionary leaders will give way to a constitutional government in any near future. But the present Nationalist movement is the result of forces which will not cease to operate, whatever may be the fate of the present leaders at Nanking. If they prove unequal to their task, other leaders will take their places, and the reconstruction of China will continue. At times, reconstruction will doubtless proceed so slowly, that observers will be unable to see that any headway is being made. Nevertheless it is likely to continue in the direction defined by the character of the Chinese Revolution heretofore. It does not seem possible that the regeneration of China by the methods Dr. Sun has taught his followers to employ can be prevented, unless exposure of the Chinese to the science of the West can be stopped, and the memory of their own political traditions blotted out. This can be predicted with confidence, since the Nationalist program, as formulated by Dr. Sun and now understood by his followers, is essentially a reconciliation of the modern political science of the West and the ancient political art of the Far East.

If it were necessary to determine now the date when the Chinese Revolution will reach the stage of constitutional government, the third of the three stages indicated in Dr. Sun's theory of revolution, one might well be in doubt about the answer to the problem of China. But this is not necessary. The ultimate fate of Dr. Sun's plans for the political reconstruction of China can be left to the future to reveal. It is sufficient for the moment to understand the general effect of Dr. Sun's plans upon the present prospects of the revolutionary movement and especially upon the stability of the political system, which is being established at Nanking. For this purpose it is enough to know that his plans, though incomplete and in part badly formulated, contain a great deal that is fundamentally sound and of excellent repute, and that his general system of political thought compares favorably with that of other great revolutionary leaders in modern times. Indeed it may be doubted whether any great revolutionary movement has been provided with a more serviceable political philosophy. The possession of such a political philosophy is a source of enduring strength to the Chinese revolutionary movement and to the political system which that movement has created. It gives the dictatorship of the Nationalist Party, the Kuomintang, a better prospect of stability than that of any other form of dictatorship that has been suggested for China.

If the dictatorship of the Kuomintang, as established at Nanking, proves durable, it is likely to endure a long time. Under the best of circumstances the educational task of the second stage in the revolutionary process, the period of tutelage, as the Chinese call it, could not be quickly accomplished. The training of the people of China for the duties of citizenship in a democratic state, and of the politicians for the duties of statesmanship, will require many years. The period of tutelage is not likely, therefore, to give way in the near future to the period of constitutional government. But this does not condemn the Revolution. The period of tutelage itself, when it shall have been definitely reached, will mark a clear advance, not only over the present period of military operations, but also over any previous period in the political development of China. The dictatorship of the Nationalist Party represents a type of political system, which is not inferior in principle to that which formerly prevailed in China, and which in practice is much better adapted to the modern world. It is not inferior in principle, because fundamentally its principles are the same. It should prove superior in practice, because its system of education is based upon modern science. The Chinese formerly possessed the requisite political capacity for successfully operating the institutions of the scholastic empire. They presumably still possess the capacity to operate the institutions, which are being planned at Nanking. Despite the quarrels of the new militarists, therefore, and the political weakness of Chinese businessmen, the outlook for the rehabilitation of China, if one does not take too short a view of the political scene, is favorable.

Confidence in the capacity of the Chinese to regenerate their state has been much shaken by the turmoil and confusion which has accompanied the overthrow of the effete Manchus and the downfall of the old-fashioned mandarins. The continuance of the turmoil and confusion under the present Nanking Government impedes the revival of confidence in Chinese political capacity. Compared to Japan or any of the strong nationalist states of the West, China seems excessively weak and disorderly. The Powers do not hesitate to remind China of their superior strength. But a comparison between China and any of the highly-centralized nationalist states is misleading. A fairer comparison is one between China and the whole of Europe, or at least the whole of Western Europe. It is not with Englishmen, Frenchmen, Germans, or Italians that Chinese should be compared, but with Europeans. Such a comparison is not so disadvantageous to China. The unification of China is certainly very imperfect. But so is that of Europe. It may take a long time for the Chinese to complete the reconstruction of their state. Or the work of reconstruction may be on the verge of rapid progress. In either event, the course of the Revolution indicates that there is no policy more promising in the long run for the tranquillity of the Far East and the peace of the world than the exercise of the necessary patience and forbearance by the Powers, while the Chinese themselves set their own house in order. Statesmen who look beyond the next presidential election or ministerial crisis at home, and all forward-looking people everywhere, will justify this policy by their confidence in the potential political capacity of the Chinese people.

INDEX

America, 6.
Arnold, Julean, 131, 133.

Bagehot, 97.
Bolshevism, effects of, in China, 62-65; *hostility of, to Christianity*, 81-83.
Borodin, 4, 89; *life and character of*, 47-48; *activities of, in China*, 50-55; *expulsion of*, 61.
Bukharin, 44.

California, University of, 3, 5.
Cantlie, Dr., 23.
Canton, 20, 37, 40, 55, 62, 139, 144.
capitalism, growth of, in China, 124-128; *moral factors in*, 128-133; *political factors in*, 133-137; *influence of, in Nationalist government*, 140-142, 145-147; *prospects for, in China*, 147-154.
Celestial Empire, government of, 11-15.
Chang Fa-kwei, 144.
Chang Tso-lin, 37, 71, 100, 102, 107, 112.
Chang Tsung-chang, 101, 113, 143.
Chiang Kai-shek, 4, 53, 138, 142, 143; *life and character of*, 108-111; *military activities of*, 111-115; *political activities of*, 115-117; *services of*, 117-122.
Chicago, 4, 47.

i